IDENTITY POLITICS IN DECONSTRUCTION

Identity politics dominates the organisation of liberation movements today. This is the case whether fighting over one's birthright to a nation, such as in the Palestinian/Israeli conflict; lobbying for civil rights, such as in gay and lesbian campaigns for marriage; or struggling for citizenry recognition as currently experienced by asylum seekers.

In this book Carolyn D'Cruz investigates the nexus between what David Birch describes as 'the seemingly impossible of high theory and the seemingly accessible possibilities of popular discourse', as encountered in liberation movements based on identity. D'Cruz reworks the logic of such movements through the unique combination of Derridean deconstruction, Foucauldian discourse and Levinasian ethics.

Moving both within and between the domains of philosophy, politics and 'postmodern culture' this book offers both a clear explication of complex philosophical issues and an understanding of how they relate to the political practicalities of everyday life.

Identity Politics in Deconstruction
Calculating with the Incalculable

CAROLYN D'CRUZ
La Trobe University, Australia

ASHGATE

Published by
Ashgate Publishing Limited
Gower House
Croft Road
Aldershot
Hampshire GU11 3HR
England

Ashgate Publishing Company
Suite 420
101 Cherry Street
Burlington, VT 05401-4405
USA

www.ashgate.com

British Library Cataloguing in Publication Data
D' Cruz, Carolyn
    Identity politics in deconstruction : calculating with the incalculable. – (Ashgate new critical thinking in philosophy)
    1. Identity (Philosophical concept) 2. Political science – Philosophy 3. Deconstruction
    I. Title
    320'.01

Library of Congress Cataloging-in-Publication Data
D' Cruz, Carolyn.
    Identity politics in deconstruction : calculating with the incalculable / Carolyn D'Cruz.
        p. cm.—(Ashgate new critical thinking in philosophy)
    ISBN 978-0-7546-6208-2 (hardcover : alk. paper)
    1. Identity (Philosophical concept) 2. Political science—Philosophy. 3. Deconstruction.
I. Title.

    BD236.D37 2008
    320.01—dc22

                                                                    2008009560

ISBN 978-0-7546-6208-2

Printed and bound in Great Britain by
TJ International Ltd, Padstow, Cornwall

For Ana, Ella and Luka

Contents

Preface

This project was first conceived in the early 1990s, a time when identity politics seemed to pervade almost all aspects of my life. During this time, the personal had become so exceedingly and painfully political in my social and professional circles that I felt caught in a never-ending loop of introductions and sharing of experiences at an AA meeting. (Hi everybody, my name is Carol, and I'm a recovering socialist feminist!) The personal articulations of the political had short-circuited for me *not* because I thought there was no place for anecdotal evidence or individual narratives in theoretical discussions of politics. No doubt, the politics of identity created a space in the academy for minority and marginalised groups to chart the ways in which personal experiences were entangled within wider relations of power and formations of knowledge. I objected to the way such entanglements collapsed into ready-made political positions. Presumptions about the status of the speaking subject, the relationship between experience and epistemology, and the correlation between theory and practice became so programmatic that there was little room left for fresh judgement and decision making when negotiating the promise for an emancipatory politics. In short, I believe that the ethical and political stakes of countersigning the heritage of the emancipatory promise toward what Derrida calls a 'democracy to come' – the primary concern of this book – would be obscured rather than enlightened by my own 'standpoint' or 'situated knowledge' in the web of power/knowledge relations.

The decision not to publicly reflect on one's own standpoint, however, goes against all inclination to follow the protocols of identity politics. Likewise, the decision to write a book that does not take up a position that either defends or denounces identity movements goes against the grain of a certain way of thinking about politics. Rather than following the protocols of identity movements, this book addresses the logic of such protocols and cautions against the perfunctory manner in which many liberation projects presume rather than interrogate the measure of progressive political theorising. In other words, this book calculates with the logic of identity politics, as it constantly confronts what unavoidably remains beyond calculation.

In recognising that the precise relations between theory and practice are not and can never be settled into a generalised formula, this book offers no easy remedy for ordering ethics, politics and philosophy into a programmatic manifesto for 'What is to be done'. This is not to flee from the responsibility to work for a more just and better world. On the contrary, it is to recognise that responding to the call for justice does not entirely belong to the order of calculability and therefore involves a vertiginous negotiation with undecidable decisions. Such recognition involves a complicated detour with questions concerning epistemology and the language of ontology – the language of what Derrida calls presence, which concerns the question of what *is*. This necessary detour in no way detracts from the urgency in which the emancipatory promise demands a response in the here and now. To reckon with the non-negotiable language of ontology that compels us to think of thought and action as oppositional predicates – even as they become undone before our very eyes – calls for greater, not less, responsibility when facing the *singularity* of all ethical and political calls to action.

Acknowledgements

My thanks to colleagues, friends and students in the area of study of Gender, Sexuality and Diversity within the School of Historical and European Studies at La Trobe University for providing a stimulating and genial environment while completing this project. I am especially grateful to Kate Brown, Jill Birch, Sarah Charters and Tom Norton at Ashgate for their fine editorial assistance. My thanks also to my friend and reading buddy, Julia Vassileva for commenting on draft chapters.

Without the support of the following people, the writing of this book would have remained beyond my reach. I owe special thanks to Niall Lucy for his crucial input at an earlier stage of this project. The spirit of our friendship and scholarly exchanges are marked throughout this book. I am very grateful to Peggy Kamuf for her insightful comments, advice on approaching the subject matter and her kind support. My brother Glenn, as always, has accompanied me in my writing process with music, humour and positive criticism. My heartfelt thanks to Glenn for reading the entire manuscript and providing constructive feedback. Above all, I thank my love, Ana, and our children, Ella and Luka. They kept me happy, gave me the space to write and showed me how to keep things in perspective.

Introduction

There is a library in Malmö, Sweden where in addition to borrowing books, you can borrow a lesbian. The list of people for loan also includes an Imam, an animal rights activist, a Gypsy, and a journalist. The rationale for this 'Living Library Project' is that a face-to-face encounter with a 'representative' of a particular identity group will go some way toward countering bigotry and preconceived stereotypes. So if you think that all lesbians are unnatural, man-hating gender inverts, a 45-minute conversation with a lesbian on loan in the library's café will expectantly inform you otherwise. Likewise, according to Ulla Brohed, spokesperson for the project, you can learn that not all animal rights activists are 'angry and intolerant', and not all journalists are 'know-it-all' and 'sensationalist'.[1] Evidently, the 'Living Library Project' extends the obvious identity markers of ethnicity, gender, sexuality and class to include political allegiances and professional occupations. The crux of the matter is that all such labels supposedly function to reinforce stereotypes that perpetuate prejudice. The struggle to overcome prejudice remains at the heart of liberation projects based on identity, so at first sight this experimental exercise in borrowing people appears more than just an amusing mechanism for raising consciousness. It seems that at least in its stated intentions, this project presumes that *knowledge* gleaned from hearing about a person's lived *experience*, will produce a more accurate picture of those subjected to, and those who embrace, particular markers of identity with a view to transforming social relations.

When I heard about this project, I could not help but wonder what would happen to library patrons interested in borrowing a lesbian if they got the likes of Sheila Jeffreys, outspoken radical lesbian feminist, as the representative spokesperson for lesbians? Well known for her anti-pornography, anti-prostitution and anti-transgender stances, Jeffreys is an Associate Professor at Melbourne University in the School of Political Science. Author of books such as *Anti-climax: A Feminist Perspective on the Sexual Revolution* (1991), *The Idea of Prostitution* (1997), *Unpacking Queer Politics: A Lesbian Feminist Perspective* (2003), and *Beauty and Misogyny: Harmful Cultural Practices in the West* (2005), Jeffreys argues that male supremacy is the cause for oppressing women and their sexuality. In her notorious pamphlet of 1973, 'Love your enemy? The Debate Between Heterosexual Feminism and Political Lesbianism', Jeffreys argued that heterosexual feminists were basically sleeping with the enemy. Thirty years later, Jeffreys revisits her argument in *Unpacking Queer Politics* by claiming that any form of penetrative sex reproduces the heteropatriarchal exploitation of women.

It is equally possible, however, that these borrowers might get a completely different loan – someone, I thought, like Pat Califia. Well known in the 1980s and

---

1   'Library offers, imam, gypsy, gay person for "loan"', 17 August 2005, accessed, 13 October 2006 http://www.abc.net.au/news/newsitems/200508/s1439257.htm.

1990s as an advocate for pornography and a writer of sadomasochist fiction, Califia then preferred to describe herself as a dyke rather than a lesbian, though, like Jeffreys, also called herself a feminist. Califia's books include erotic fiction such as *Macho Sluts* (1989) and *No Mercy* (2000) as well as non-fiction, such as *Sapphistry: The Book of Lesbian Sexuality* (1988) and *Sex Changes: The Politics of Transgenderism* (1997). To get up to speed on Califia's latest works, I Googled her only to find that Pat has become Patrick, who now identifies as a bisexual transgendered person. There is always room for reclassifications in a library, in language and in life.

The point of reflecting on these hypothetical borrowing situations reveals at least two things: first, identities can and do change, but secondly, and more importantly, *any* identity marker is bound to contain *internal divisions* that make it impossible to settle coherently on a definitive representative. Such internal divisions would be familiar to any one engaged in identity politics, where markers such as gender, race, sexuality, class, and nation attempt to maintain their grounds as fundamental organising principles from which to position theoretical perspectives and political strategies for changing relations of powers. What is both striking and appealing about the 'Living Library Project' is that it focuses on the singular face-to-face encounter between a self and other, an encounter that Emmanuel Levinas describes in a radically different context as the ethical relation. We will have further recourse to this relation later in the book. Unlike the 'Living Library Project', however, identity politics largely articulate themselves and operate on the level of collectivist and mass movements.

Whether fighting over one's 'birthright' to a nation, such as in the Palestinian/ Israeli conflict, demonstrating for one's civil rights, such as in the recent gay and lesbian campaign for marriage, or struggling for recognition for the right to asylum, appeals to identity continue to dominate the organisation of liberation movements in society today. Notwithstanding the popularity of identity politics, the means by which such movements authenticate identity formations, devise strategies for identifying and subverting relations of powers, and develop processes for negotiating troubled interactions between philosophy, politics and ethics are far from transparent and innocent. The same impossible ideals that plagued earlier left-wing projects trouble the politics of identities. Namely, the impracticable venture to found a collective agent for social change, an inability to remain uncontaminated by the very powers such movements aim to subvert, and the incapacity to reconcile disjunctions between theory, practice and ethics. This is to say, the prevalence of identity politics, betrays insurmountable philosophical complexities and tactical problems these movements face in articulating and affecting agendas for their emancipatory ideals. We could say that the Jeffreys and Califia problem is multiplied on a much larger scale here. This is not news to many of those involved in identity politics. The 1980s and 1990s were tumultuous decades for these movements, when identity movements occupied centre stage in debates about political correctness, and the so-called wars concerning culture, theory and history.[2] These two decades saw much-needed philosophical and

---

2   See J. Williams ed., *PC Wars: Politics and Theory in the Academy* (New York: Routledge, 1995). This compilation features a series of essays by 'public intellectuals' who discuss PC in the context of the American Academy. For a concise genealogy of PC and for

political critique of identity politics, forcing these movements to confront the inherent fault lines in their presumed foundations. What had been inspirational movements in the 1960s era of civil liberties, and had found public voice in affirmative action and equal opportunity practices in the 1970s and early 1980s began showing cracks in theoretical frameworks guiding the emancipatory ideal, and producing fights, factionalism and fragmentation within the political ranks of those organising these movements. The question thus remains: how can identity politics manifest and rearticulate itself for the twenty-first century? And are such forms of political organisation congruent with these movements' emancipatory aims?

Recent literature on identity politics calls for reclaiming and reconsidering identity against what Linda Alcoff describes as an 'a priori repudiation' of it.[3] Adopting the category of 'post-positivist realists', contemporary self-identified 'intellectual activists' defend identity politics in response to questions raised by what they call 'postmodernist deconstructions of such key concepts as identity, experience, and knowledge.'[4] As debates over the last twenty years or so testify, the nebulous taxonomy of 'postmodernism' and its alleged alliance to the equally dubious categorisation of deconstruction evidently shed serious doubt on the philosophical and political import of identity and all its related concepts. Yet, as is so often the case, the propensity for position taking in such debates prevented many commentators in the field from actually engaging with the *singularity* of particular philosophers associated with postmodernism and deconstruction. Instead, the logic of 'for or against' arguments seized the terms of debate in which the politics of identity and the identity of the political could be examined. Specifically, there is a clearly discernible trend in arguments concerned with identity politics to either defend or denounce the status of identity, postmodernism, essentialism, foundationalism, and so on.

This book departs from such position taking in debates about identity politics and political correctness insofar as it argues *neither* for *nor* against such movements and all their related polemics. Instead, this study inserts itself within some of the more salient polemics within the field in order to *shift the approach and terms of debate* in which current commentaries seem compelled to conform. Such an approach follows the lead primarily of French thinkers, Jacques Derrida, Michel Foucault and, as earlier mentioned, Emmanuel Levinas. Of the three thinkers, proponents of identity politics are most receptive to Foucault. At first sight, Foucault's work far more readily lends itself to rethinking an accepted idea of progressive politics, and

---

a collection of responses by various academics negotiating the impact within the university, see R. Feldstein, *Political Correctness: A Response from the Cultural Left* (Minneapolis and London: University of Minnesota Press, 1997). For a more complex analysis of the constitution of the 'public' in these debates see, P. Kamuf, *The Division of Literature or the University in Deconstruction* (Chicago and London: The University of Chicago Press, 1997), pp. 133–61. For a commentary on importation of the media 'PC Panic' and the Australian academy, see D. Bennett, 'PC Panic, The Press and the Academy', *Meanjin: Cultural Difference and its Enemies*, 3 (Spring 1993): 435–46.

   3   L. Alcoff, *Visible Identities Race, Gender and The Self* (Oxford: Oxford University Press, 2006), p. 85.

   4   L. M. Alcoff, M. R. Hames-García, S. P. Mohanty and P. M. L. Moya (eds), *Identity Politics Reconsidered* (New York: Palgrave, 2006), p. 4.

appears to bypass some of the more philosophically challenging critiques of identity regarding foundations of knowledge and essentialism. The opening chapters of the book explore Foucault's attempt to disentangle politics from metaphysics; they also demonstrate how useful such analyses can still be to a certain form of transformative politics.

Yet, as revitalising as a Foucauldian approach might be, his commitment to the emancipatory ideal can unwittingly foreclose what both Derrida and Levinas see as an opening toward the Other. Unfortunately, the status of the Other has acquired a somewhat clichéd circulation amongst discourses of identity politics, prompting yet another camping on positions between proponents and critics. Recognising the concern that there is a 'knee jerk appeal' to the Other when identity is at issue,[5] Dominick La Capra drolly remarks, 'Whenever I hear "identity," I reach for my inner alterity'.[6] Of course, knee jerk reactions ought to be met with suspicion, but that does not mean that the question raised – alterity in this case–is not crucial to the issue at hand – identity. The problem here concerns the haste and generality in reaching and articulating a philosophico-political position rather than dealing with the ineluctable confrontation between identity and alterity itself.

Derrida's approach to identity and alterity resists generalisation into a 'position', which evidently earns deconstruction a bad name in politics. Understandably, though erroneously, the measure of a progressive 'political philosophy' has become entangled with calls for philosophers to set out political programmes to guide the making of ethico-political decisions and meet the demand of immediate accessibility and applicability for political interventions. Yet, the transformative potential that Derrida's deconstruction in particular can bring to the emancipatory promise of identity politics is not immediately discernible, easily understood, or readily applicable as it were. Moreover, the activist call to the academy, a call that initially inspired my own studies, is to find ways to make theory and practice fit, and to reconcile disjunctures between politics, philosophy and ethics. This is a difficult and interminable problem facing any politics in any time and in any place. Derrida's own treatment of these troubled relations requires a novel way of thinking, which does not march to the same rhythm of many 'intellectual activists' on the left – particularly those concerned with identity.

What the generality of an introduction cannot demonstrate, but the detail of each chapter can, is that programmatic responses to political standoffs can obstruct and neutralise the imperative to actually think and take responsibility for the singular *act* of making an ethico-political decision. Furthermore, the demand for accessibility and applicability can permanently defer and deter necessary negotiations with complex forms of theorising, whose immediate 'uses' might be difficult to discern, but whose enduring implications for the pursuit of emancipatory ideals remain imperative.

---

5   See L. Alcoff, 'Who's Afraid of Identity Politics?', in P. M. L. Moya and M. R. Hames-García (eds), *Reclaiming Identity Politics, Realist Theory and the Predicament of Postmodernism* (California: University of California Press, 2000), pp. 312–44

6   D. La Capra, 'Experience and Identity', in L. M. Alcoff, M. R. Hames-García, S. P. Mohanty and P. M. L. Moya (eds), *Identity Politics Reconsidered* (Palgrave: New York, 2006), pp. 228–45. This quotation, p. 244.

There is growing evidence that a more nuanced articulation of identity politics is developing with regard to these issues in recent years. Nevertheless, what stubbornly continues to drive recent articulations of identity politics is the effort to *reconcile* the *disjointure* between theory and practice by presupposing these categories as reducible to one another. This is to say, identity movements find it difficult to hear that an emphasis on reconciling disjunctions between ethics, politics, and philosophy can forbid a reckoning not only with the inescapability of facing the irreducibility between theory and practice, but also with the *necessity of this lack of accord* as a means for keeping open to the future of emancipatory promise itself. For both Derrida and Levinas, this opening is necessary for what they view as the 'incoming of the Other'.

Of course, in the form of a slogan, 'the incoming of the Other' and the emphasis on disjointure may leave some proponents of identity politics with little desire to read any further. For despite the many commentators who have painstakingly tried to correct the view that deconstruction is bad news for a progressive politics, suspicion and disdain for examining identity politics in deconstruction remains. According to a certain logic driving these movements, Derrida's works do not 'measure up' to popular demands for political and intellectual activism. Responding to this popular view, I argue – as have other Derrida scholars before me – that the very concept of the political here needs urgent re-examination. My specific intervention of rethinking the political pertains to the emancipatory promise as it is articulated within discourses of identity politics, which desperately needs deconstruction. In fact, *identity politics are already in deconstruction*, a fact that happens, as John Caputo is fond of saying, with or without Jacques Derrida.[7]

The many splits and controversies over who can be included in what category of identity, over how to represent the politically and socially marginal, and over how to negotiate lived experiences in the empirical world with ideals to change the world, all sit on the fault lines of the 'ungrounded' grounds of identity politics. In other words, deconstructive strategies of reading and writing not merely expose, but importantly *work otherwise* what is already there. Identities, understandings of experience, and foundations of knowledge are fractured from the start, and in acknowledging the faulty logic of binary oppositions at the heart of all such origins, deconstruction aims to work with, rather than deny, the collisions and crises between and within all the oppositional predicates inhering in the articulation and elaboration of the emancipatory promise. So rather than focusing on what can secure the impossible grounds of identity politics, the focus here is on what issues have exposed these fault lines and brought such a politics into crisis. Contrary to what critics of deconstruction might think such a focus does not lead to political paralysis and quietism.

One way of describing deconstruction's exposure of such fault lines and deconstruction in general is as 'the experience of the impossible'.[8] Such an experience might involve questioning the foundations of metaphysics and antithetical values

---

7   See J. Captuo, *Against Ethics: Contributions to a Poetics of Obligations with Constant Reference to Deconstruction* (Indianapolis: Indiana University Press, 1993).

8   The phrase appears in J. Derrida, 'Force of Law: "The Mystical Foundation of Authority"', trans. M. Quaintance in *Deconstruction and the Possiblity of Justice*, eds

at the very same time as acknowledging an indebtedness and unavoidable reliance on such thinking. With regard to the emancipatory promise, such an experience of the impossible might involve confronting all the empirical evidence that no singular or collective identity can meet the transcendental ideal of the emancipatory subject. For example, neither Sheila Jeffreys nor the former Pat, or present Patrick, Califia could fulfil the function of representing the emancipatory subject for lesbians. Whatever the case – whether aiming to name the emancipatory subject or define exactly how politics and philosophy relate to one another – the experience involves reaching an impassable or impossible path, a path that Derrida calls an aporia. At the point of an aporia the logic of for and against arguments, or yes or no position taking, reaches a point of exhaustion. A new kind of logic is called for. This book aims to open discourses of identity politics to this call.

Across five chapters, the book engages with five interconnected questions regularly encountered in debates concerning struggles over identities. Each chapter progressively moves toward the emancipatory promise related to what Derrida calls a democracy to come.

'What Matter Who's Speaking?'

Chapter 1 deals with the question of representation, and the matter of who can legitimately speak about what. As the panic around political correctness reached a peak late last century, so did the practice of declaring one's identity markers. Identity markers alone became a shorthand signal for situating oneself and one's knowledge claims in relation to others. Whether attending political rallies, going to conference papers, or writing journal articles and books in relation to identity politics, the autobiographical practice of declaring one's identity took hold as the most common way of introducing one's political and critical credentials. As opening declarations about one's speaking position – speaking as 'as a white, working class, gay man, for instance' – became more lengthy and preposterous (a conference paper was once opened with a woman declaring to the audience that she ate pussy), critique on identity politics revealed more about the author's biography than the issues at stake. While personal revelations may sometimes be relevant, they are often treated in too perfunctory a manner within discourses of identity movements.

The first chapter follows Foucault's methods for examining those rules and procedures that come into play whenever proponents of identity politics assess the legitimacy of knowledge claims by recourse to markers of identity. The analysis proceeds by examining a case study whose subject matter is particularly sensitive: namely the status of speaking positions in a debate conducted in the journal *Oceania* about definitions of Aboriginal identities in Australia. As this chapter makes clear, the link between the authentication of one's identity and the legitimation of knowledges based on that authentication is less transparent than many of the contributors to debates about identity suppose.

D. Cornell, M. Rosenfeld and D. G. Carlson (New York and London: Routledge, 1992), pp. 3–67. This quotation, p. 15.

Between Epistemology and Experience

Chapter 2 is concerned with the question of foundations and looks more closely at debates about privileging experience as an ontological ground for articulating identity politics. As essentialist assumptions concerning the unity of an identity have been increasingly questioned in the academy, ways of locating the origins of oppression, writing the 'lost' histories of subjugated identities and formulating strategies for subverting dominant relations of powers are being reframed accordingly. This shift in theorising identity has raised issues regarding the epistemic status of subjectivity. Specifically, I track the endurance of debates to the present day that first emerged from Joan Scott's critique of the 'evidence of experience' in the early 1990s. Such debate belongs to the wider context in which the Foucauldian concept of discourse challenged the political potency of valued oppositions such as truth and ideology when theorising social transformation. This chapter reaches a point that calls for more refined and stratified distinctions between sites of intervention – such as curriculum content and research – as well as for enhanced differentiation between orders of analysis – such as politics and philosophy – when subjugated identities are at issue.

In exploring how various commentators have struggled to situate the truth of experience in furthering the goals of identity movements, debate turns to questions of foundations and metaphysics. While present forms of this debate mostly situate critics as belonging to either a realist or postmodernist position, I argue that this obfuscates important differences between Foucault and Derrida in particular. Such differences alter the very *grounds* upon which identity movements can presume to stake their claims for the emancipatory promise. As such, the seemingly abstract questions of metaphysics implicate a radical rethinking of what we presume to be concrete materiality when making political decisions.

Choosing One's Heritage: Between philosophy and politics

Chapter 3 takes its point of departure from Karl Marx's famous Thesis XI: 'Philosophers have interpreted the world in various ways; the point however is to change it.'[9] It examines the desire to reconcile politics with philosophy, and focuses on conflicts inhering in our necessary negotiation with the language of ontology – the language of 'what is' – as we struggle to realise the emancipatory promise in praxis. In responding to the heritage of the Enlightenment ideal to link truth to liberty via Kant and Foucault's reading of the former, I affirm a particular legacy that also informs present articulations of identity politics. I follow this link between truth and liberty through to Derrida's reading of Marx, which involves rethinking the alleged oppositions between the material and ideal worlds as manifest in the signifiers of communism and democracy during the Cold War. In learning that neither the philosophical nor the political can claim supremacy in setting agendas for social change, this chapter forces a confrontation with the necessity

---

9 K. Marx, 'Theses on Feuerbach', trans. G. Benton in *Early Writings: Marx* (Harmondsworth: Penguin, 1974), pp. 421–3. Thesis XI appears on p. 423 [G. 1845].

of working with *the irreducibility between politics and philosophy* for the future of the emancipatory promise. That the Cold War has been displaced by the 'War against Terrorism' reinforces rather than detracts from aligning Derrida's inventive approach to (re)thinking the emancipatory promise in terms of a 'democracy to come'. As the philosophical complexity increases for rethinking identity politics in terms of a democracy to come, the terrain upon which such movements elaborate their emancipatory ideals are asked to shift toward a non-programmable politics in the name of an ethical opening toward the Other.

Truth, Law and Justice: Responding to the stolen generations in the disadjusted time of the present

Chapter 4 turns to the question of ethics and justice by drawing on the works of both Levinas and Derrida. Emphasising the irreducibility rather than substitutability between the concepts of law and justice, Derrida's critique of presence scrutinises the inclination within discourses of identity politics to seek recourse for justice by prioritising legislative change in struggles for social transformation. Following Derrida's focus on the gap between law and justice is not to suggest that we should not pursue legal struggles, but to question the assumption that law can comprehensively calculate justice. To consider the interval between law and justice more closely, this chapter looks through the lens of recent controversies over the status of the 'stolen generations' of Aboriginal people in Australia and the issue of 'forgiveness' regarding past injustices. Not only does the issue question the status of the 'present' in legal terms, but it becomes clear that calls for justice, through the ethical relation, come to us through countless *singular* idioms, which interrupt and penetrate the reification of law as the foundation of universal human rights. To demand that law negotiate with the incalculability of singular calls from incoming others offers a constructive criticism for identity politics. For such calls allow a shift from ontological and political questions to the question of ethics. This question of ethics demands that any struggle based on an identity marker has a responsibility to those others that might come before the law or remain beneath the law. This is certainly the case with the stolen generations, and continues to operate wherever legal identity papers fall below recognition.

Welcome Stranger: Democracy 'to come', Autoimmunity and Hospitality

Chapter 5 embraces the turn toward the domain of ethics as it is the space of ethics that calls us to responsibility and sets in motion the tension between philosophy and politics. Yet the domain of the ethical in the Levinasian sense is undermined by the propensity for identity movements to *calculate* their struggles in terms of the concepts of freedom and equality associated with a *determined* concept of democracy (in the form of a nation state) and an inclination to protect their own sovereignty (in the form of an identity marker). By situating sovereignty and democracy as inscribed by an autoimmune process – a process 'where a living being, in quasi suicidal fashion, "itself" works to destroy its own protection, to immunize itself against its "own" immunity',[10] this chapter turns to the figure of the refugee as offering identity politics a ground breaking twist, which exposes the impossible grounds of securing a collective emancipatory subject. For as important as the order of calculability is for ensuring the democratic struggle for 'equality of citizens before the law', the refugee reminds us that the principle of democracy is also committed to remaining open to the 'incalculable singularity of any one'.[11] This issue opens onto the question of hospitality, following Derrida's consideration of whether it is necessary to ask the other as foreigner or stranger to verify his or her identity before a welcome is extended. The figure of the refugee, the foreigner and stranger leave identity movements with the question of confronting the necessary tension between hostility and hospitality to those others that remain outside their own orders of calculability.

While it is clear from the outset that this book does not offer a *programme* for how identity based movements ought to negotiate a democratic future this does not mean that the emancipatory ideals of such movements are set aside. Such an assumption is far from the case. In arguing that a programmatic politics can too readily lend itself to hasty judgement in tackling the murky issues that propel the protocols and procedures for articulating and enacting identity movements, this book aims to shift the parameters in which debates about the politics of identity and the identity of politics can take place. In calculating with the protocols and logic operating through discourses of identity politics, I hope to open such discourses to the necessity of taking into consideration that which remains beyond calculability. This does make a difference to how politics relates to ethical decisions and thus ultimately makes a difference to how we can maintain the promise for social transformation as being more open rather than closed to an emancipatory future.

---

10 J. Derrida, 'Autoimmunity: Real and Symbolic Suicide', in *Philosophy in a Time of Terror*, ed. G. Borradori (Chicago, IL: University of Chicago Press, 2003), pp. 85–136. This quotation, p. 94.

11 J. Derrida, *Rogues: Two Essays on Reason* (Stanford, CA: Stanford University Press, 2005), p. 120.

Chapter One

'What Matter Who's Speaking?'[1]

Rhetorical question: A question to which no answer is expected
(The American Heritage Dictionary)

Rhetorical questions: asked not for information but to produce effect, as who cares? For nobody cares.
(The Concise Oxford Dictionary)

Identity politics cannot function without the underlying assumption that it very much matters who I am, who you are, and what possibilities are open to, or closed for, us in order to form a 'we'. To ask the rhetorical question 'What Matter Who's Speaking?' in a book about identity politics might therefore seem absurd. For the rhetorical register of the question – What matter? For it matters little – fosters a dismissive tone toward identity. Yet the grammatical pattern disallows the figurative meaning to gain precedence as the only meaning to the question. The literal meaning remains within the structure of the sentence.[2] And, as anyone who has been active within identity politics would know, the propensity within such movements is to answer literally why it very much matters who is speaking. Advocates of identity politics might even suggest that only those who enjoy the privilege of *not* being marked by a marginalised identity can entertain the rhetorical register. To put this in the parlance of identity politics, supposedly only a white, middle class man can afford to attend to rhetoric and contemplate the *undecidability* between the two meanings inhering in the same sentence. In the realm of politics, so the logic goes, there is no time for attending to such undecidability. But, this undecidability is not only a grammatical issue; it is also a political one. As I argue in this chapter, each meaning might bear its own appropriateness within a specific context and order of analysis.

It is not easy, however, to attain a position from which to reflect upon the undecidability between the literal and figurative meanings of the question. More often than not, *before confronting any other qualifying prerequisite to speak* we must satisfy the criteria of bearing the marker of identity that is spoken about. So presumably, only women can speak about women's issues, only those belonging to a specific ethnic minority can speak on behalf of that particular group, and so on. Following Foucault's attention to the figurative meaning of the question, the present chapter reflects on the limiting, and sometimes dangerous, effects of

---

1   M. Foucault quoting S. Beckett in 'What is an Author?,' trans. D. F. Bouchard and S. Simon, in *Language, Counter Memory and Practice: Selected Essays and Interviews by Michel Foucault*, ed. D. F. Bouchard (New York: Cornell University Press, 1977), p. 138.

2   See P. de Man, 'Semiology and Rhetoric', in *Allegories of Reading: Figural Language in Rousseau, Nietzsche, Rilke, and Proust* (New Haven, CT: Yale University Press, 1979).

categorically instituting such a prerequisite. This involves treating the status of the concrete speaking subject as secondary to the *function* of the speaking *position* from which a concrete subject finds that she or he *must* speak. In other words, the matter of speaking is to be examined first without a concrete 'who'. Within Foucault's archaeological analysis, the status of the concrete speaking subject is not at issue. At issue instead are the rules and procedures – which must be followed – that regulate discourse. Such rules and procedures must be in place before granting any concrete subject validity and legitimacy in speaking.

This chapter addresses the particular protocol of speaking rights by way of examining a specific debate about 'Aboriginal'[3] identities in Australia. The debate took place in the late 1992 and early 1993 issues of *Oceania* – a journal identifying itself with the 'field of social and cultural anthropology [whose] primary regional orientation is to the indigenous peoples of Australia, Melanesia, Polynesia, Micronesia, and South East Asia'.[4] It erupted after a self-identified non-Aboriginal teacher of Aboriginal Studies, David Hollinsworth, attempted to evaluate various 'discourses of Aboriginality ... in terms of their apparent implications for Aboriginal political struggles'. Unsurprisingly, many participants in the debate question the legitimacy of Hollinsworth's right to do so. At the same time, however, most participants themselves are seemingly intent on articulating a *position* regarding the merits of different definitions of Aboriginal identity and claims to authenticity. In various public spaces in Australia debates about both issues – the right to speak and the question concerning what constitutes authentic Aboriginal identity – occur with impassioned regularity. The issue also links, albeit it in a complex way, to the political goal for self-determination within Aboriginal communities. Self-determination requires self-representation, which suggests that a subjugated group must be allowed to speak on their own behalf. Lack of consultation and representation of Aboriginal people within government policies and practices has worsened rather than improved living conditions in these communities.[5]

---

3   As pointed out later in the chapter, the category of Aboriginal person homogenises the diversity of peoples identified in indigenous regional terms such as Koori, Nyoongah, Wongi, Murris, to name a few. I begin by using the term Aboriginal peoples because I will be referring to a debate that discusses Australian Aboriginal identity in general.

4   I am referring to the following articles that appeared over two issues of *Oceania:* D. Hollinsworth, 'Discourses on Aboriginality and the Politics of Identity in Australia', *Oceania*, 63, 2 (1992): 137–55; M. Nyoongah, 'Self-determining Our Aboriginality, A Response to "Discourses on Aboriginality and the Politics of Identity in Urban Australia"', *Oceania*, 63, 2 (1992): 156–7; B. Attwood, 'Comment on Hollinsworth', *Oceania*, 63, 2 (1992): 158–9; A. Lattas, 'Wiping the Blood off Aboriginality: The Politics of Aboriginal Embodiment in Contemporary Intellectual Debate', *Oceania*, 63, 2 (1992): 160–64; J. Beckett, 'Comment on Hollinsworth', *Oceania*, 63, 2 (1992): 165–7; D. Hollinsworth, 'Coagulating Categories: A Reply to Responses', *Oceania*, 63, 2 (1992): 168–71; G. Cowlishaw, 'Introduction: Representing Racial Issues', *Oceania*, 63, 3 (1993): 183–94; A. Lattas, 'Essentialism, Memory and Resistance: Aboriginality and the Politics of Authenticity', *Oceania*, 63, 3 (1993): 240–67.

5   During the course of writing this book, the previous Federal Government declared a 'national emergency' to address issues of child sexual abuse within Aboriginal communities in

The issue of representation and legitimacy also relates to the matter of determining the authenticity of Aboriginal art, where revelations of fraudulent artists not only dramatically drop the market value of the paintings at issue, but raise questions about what makes authenticity discernible. Similarly, in other contexts, questions of Aboriginal authenticity persistently arise when negotiating representations of Aboriginal people to various publics, whether they are portrayals of Aboriginal people in the media, film, museums, education curriculums and other aspects of cultural life. And as Aboriginal people are forced to continue the colonial legacy of negotiating with 'official' governmental definitions of their identity for bureaucratic purposes, there is no shortage of public opinion – particularly on talkback radio and letters to the editor in newspapers – pronouncing criterion for determining what ought to constitute an authentic Aboriginal person.

In all forms of this debate, there is a tendency to reduce the complexity of the issues at stake, *firstly*, to a choice between two polarised political positions: either it does matter who speaks or it does not. Of course, this matter is important, but there is an impulsive proclivity to reduce all argument to the identity of the subject doing the speaking. Before any further discussion about authenticity can take place it is worthwhile considering more closely the problems and issues conditioning the legitimacy of the speaking subject. The *Oceania* debate provides a fertile ground from which to do so, as the issues raised are as relevant to today's history wars as discussed in Chapter Four as they are to examining everyday negotiations of Aboriginal identity in past, present and future discussions. It cannot be overstated that the present chapter reviews the *Oceania* debate by *not* taking up an either/or position over the matter of speaking. Rather it explores *various positions* from which subjects are constrained and enabled to speak when negotiating what Foucault calls the 'formidable materiality of discourse'.[6] In doing so, the debate on the matter of speaking and the related problem of authenticity will not be resolved to the binary positions that either it matters or it does not matter who speaks, or that Aboriginality means this or that. Rather the chapter is interested in how possibilities for political interventions can be multiplied and become more specified and understood in their singularity.

Speaking positions, power and knowledge

Some participants' comments in the *Oceania* discussion suggest that the politics of speaking positions is, in fact, self-evident. Not surprisingly, a large point of

---

the Northern Territory. In taking direct control of the affairs of local Aboriginal communities, the Federal Government ignored the recommendation from the Northern Territory commissioned report, *Little Children Are Scared*, to involve and consult with Aboriginal communities in developing responsive policy. For a critique of the intervention from a number of contributors, see J. Altman and M. Hinkson, *Coercive Reconciliation: Stabilise, Normalise, Exit Aboriginal Australia* (Melbourne: Arena Publications, 2007).

6   M. Foucault, 'The Order of Discourse', trans. I. McLeod, in Robert Young (ed.), *Untying the Text: A Post-Structuralist Reader* (Boston: Routledge and Kegan Paul, 1981), pp. 51–77.

contention centres on the right of non-Aboriginal people to speak about Aboriginal identities and issues. This effectively sets the frame from which to discuss the matter of speaking in terms that *must* connect the identity of the investigating subject with the identity of the object/subject in question. Put more simply, we cannot view the speaker as a disinterested or impartial observer of the issues in question. Accordingly, each speaker presumably enters some kind of power relationship with the investigated identity in the act of participating in the debate. Now this might seem obvious. Such recognition is evident in the widespread compulsion for speakers and writers to declare a list of their own identity markers – such as skin colour, gender, race, sexuality, political allegiance and so on – as some kind of shorthand signal for situating themselves and their knowledge claims in relation to others. (For instance, film theorist E. Ann Kaplan asks 'How can I enter or approach the culture of Aborigines, as a white Anglo-Celt who has lived long in North America?'[7])

Sometimes the declaration is used to problematise the speaking subject's 'right' to speak about the particular identity in question (such as a non-Aboriginal person speaking about issues pertaining to Aboriginal identity); at other times, the declaration acts as some kind of verifier for what is being said. The former use of the declaration emphasises the desire not to speak on behalf of, or with authority about, another culture, and to recognise the imbalance of power relations in an encounter between dominant and marginalised identities. The latter use seemingly encourages the view that knowledge claims are reducible to, and locatable within, the 'authenticity' of a particular identity's subjective experience. An extreme version of the latter use occurs when a speaking subject's knowledge claims, concerning an alleged constitution of social reality, are evaluated on the basis of his or her identity markers. Unfortunately, these three issues concerning the speaking subject – the problem of speaking on behalf of, and about, others; the claim that knowledge can be reduced to a subject's experience; and the claim that knowledge can be legitimated with recourse to the mere marker of an identity – are often left undifferentiated when debating the matter of representation within discourses of identity politics. This chapter aims to open ways for disentangling the conflation of these three positions.

The status of the speaking subject in the *Oceania* debate

In one form or another, each participant in the *Oceania* debate abides by the practice of 'situating' his or her knowledges by disclosing their own markers of identity, or at least their own perceived qualifications to contribute to, or refrain from, discussing Aboriginal authenticity. It seems that if the investigating subject's identity coincides with the identity of the subject in question, then this person has a more legitimate perspective from which to speak. The following is a list of the forms in which participants disclose their identities:

---

7   E. Ann Kaplan quoted in M. Langton, 'Well I Heard it on the Radio and I saw it on the Television: an Essay for the Australian Film Commission on the Politics and Aesthetics of Filmmaking by and about Aboriginal People and Things' (Woolloomooloo: Australian Film Commission, 1993), p. 24.

As a non-Aboriginal person who has taught Aboriginal Studies to both Aboriginal and non-Aboriginal tertiary students, these arguments are of intense significance, professionally, personally, and politically.[8]

I believe that such a search and any conclusions reached must come from us, ourselves. We must determine our own identity within the parameters established by us.[9]

I could also question in itself the politics of a white person (like Hollinsworth) seeking to police the collective memories through which Aborigines invent and reclaim a measure of their authenticity.[10]

In calling upon Aborigines to undertake thoroughly the work of historicising themselves ... it is axiomatic that in the production of their history Aborigines do not embrace the generalised and one-dimensional history created by non-Aboriginal historians or anthropologists but instead follow the practice of those Aboriginal autobiographers who have more ably engaged with the complex specificity of their pasts.[11]

For my part, I shall not presume to advise Aboriginal people about how to articulate an identity. . .[12]

I do not consider my position as an educated white bourgeois woman, sharing more of the experiences of the do-gooders and blow-ins than of the Blacks in Bourke, Katherine, Redfern, or Arnhem Land, as a disabling analytical perspective, especially in relation to issues of racism.[13]

These declarations – though quite varied – supposedly situate each author's qualifications, or political suitability, for entering the matter concerning 'the means of claiming, contesting and authenticating Aboriginal identity'.[14]

Ironically, Hollinsworth investigates the very category seen as legitimising one's speaking position ('Aboriginality') for its possible exclusionary boundaries. Crucially, however, the exclusions to which the debate directs its attention concern Aboriginal inscriptions of identity only; some Aboriginal identities are perceived to bear greater claims to authenticity than others. This issue prompts Hollinsworth to open the discussion. His aim is to question various 'discourses' that attempt to define what constitutes a person's Aboriginality, as he believes that some definitions in circulation have a tendency to create a hierarchy of Aboriginal authenticity. For example, he claims that many urban Aborigines have experienced instances in which their own identities are considered less authentic than rural Aborigines. Of course contesting the authenticity of Aboriginal identity is not only a problem for some of the students Hollinsworth engages with as a teacher in Aboriginal studies. Such contestations repeatedly air on talkback radio and appear in letters to the editor in

8   Hollinsworth, 'Discourses on Aboriginality', p. 137.
9   Nyoongah, 'Self-determining our Aboriginality', p. 156.
10 Lattas, 'Wiping the Blood of Aboriginality', p. 160.
11 Attwood, 'Comment on Hollinsworth', p. 159.
12 Beckett, 'Comment on Hollinsworth', p. 165.
13 Cowlishaw, 'Introduction: Representing Racial Issues', p. 183.
14 Hollinsworth, 'Discourses on Aboriginality', p. 137.

the popular press. Needless to say, refutations of authenticity help fuel the racist rhetoric of conservative lobbyists whose mission is to abolish welfare provisions for Aboriginal people, whom they do not consider to be 'real' Aborigines. As Hollinsworth remarks, 'the means of claiming, contesting and authenticating Aboriginal identity are central to both the future of Aboriginal Studies as an academic area of study and to political and ideological struggles over Australian nationalism and the position of indigenous peoples within it'.[15] For Hollinsworth then his professional, personal and political stakes regarding the issue compel him to speak. In suspending a verdict over whether Hollinsworth had the right to do so – that is the right to speak about definitions of Aboriginal identity – let us first see if we can shift the terms of the debate by employing Foucault's tools for an archaeological analysis of discourse.[16] This will better position us to reconsider the status of the speaking subject.

An archaeological approach to 'representing' Aboriginal identity

In the context of the frantic debates around postmodernism and the subject of identity politics, Foucault's positioning of the (speaking) subject as an effect of discourse had become misleadingly simplified to the erroneous idea that there is no materiality to subjectivity. Such an idea must maintain a rigid opposition between materiality and ideality, and assume that discourse belongs to the realm of ideas, while identities belong to the empirical, material world. Let us suspend for now an examination of the complex relations between the material and ideal – such questions will be visited in the following two chapters – and consider Foucault's contention that his concept of discourse exerts a certain materiality over subjectivity. This is to say, for Foucault, it is not that subjectivity has no materiality, but that alongside the social conditions of existence that according to a certain logic of identity politics constitute a person's identity (such as race, economic status, sex, nation, education and so on), one ought to include the 'formidable materiality of discourse'.

While Hollinsworth situates his paper in terms of a discussion of 'discourses of Aboriginality', he does not take 'discourse' to exert a materiality in the Foucauldian sense. For Foucault, 'discourse belongs to the order of laws', *where a place is made ready for a subject to speak.*[17] As he explains: '[w]e know quite well that we do not have the right to say everything, that we cannot speak of just anything in any circumstances whatever, and that not everyone has the right to speak of anything whatever'.[18] Consequently, to examine discourses of Aboriginal identity politics in Australia in the Foucauldian sense, we would be interested in describing the rules and procedures that regulate what constrains and what can enable what can be spoken of, how the speaking must take place, and who can do the speaking. Put another way, discourse refers to the practice of *how* we can say *what* we say *about* particular objects with legitimacy. In turning to the rules and procedures regulating

---

15 Holllinsworth, p. 137.

16 M. Foucault, *The Archaeology of Knowledge*, trans. A. M. Sheridan Smith (London and New York: Tavistock, 1972) [Fr 1969].

17 Foucault, 'The Order of Discourse', p. 51.

18 Ibid., p. 52.

discursive practices, Foucault's archaeological analysis aims to avoid reducing the history of ideas and history 'proper' to either a transcendental or an empirical subject of consciousness. With the emphasis shifted from these two models of subjectivity, Foucault argues attending to the materiality of discourse is not concerned with interpreting the intentions behind meaning by referring to the concrete speaking subject. Rather, he proposes to subvert the conventional role assigned to the founding and creative subject.

Accordingly, an archaeological approach is less concerned with the *right* for a concrete subject to speak, than it is with the *place made ready* – within a specific institutional site and discursive practice – for a *variety* of concrete subjects to occupy the *very same position*. Thus in an academic journal, in which the issue of identity politics is raised, all participants in the *Oceania* debate have varied identities, but each appears compelled to follow the protocol of situating his or her own identity markers as they speak. Alternatively, the same concrete subject can occupy a variety of different speaking positions depending on the institutional site and discursive practice in which that speaking takes place. Thus, if Hollinsworth were presenting his case to talkback radio instead of an academic journal he would have had to articulate his arguments in lay person's terms. He would also need to account for the probability of speaking to some racists in the audience, and he would need to be aware of the editing processes that affect and effect his speech on live to air radio.[19] In such a context, footnotes and academic evidence to support his argument are not relevant. And as there are institutional variations effecting the site of the speaking subject, so are there such variations effecting definitions of identity.

Hollinsworth aims to evaluate different definitions in terms of their political efficacy, as is outlined below. But for an archaeological analysis the issue is not so much concerned with adjudicating between better denotations of identities as it is with mapping different circulations in which identities are claimed. Hence examining the speaking subject in terms of discourse is not to deny a materiality to subjectivity, but to show that the materiality of subjectivity has no fixed essence. Speaking about an identity without fixing that identity as having an unchanging meaning in time and space has prompted many proponents of identity politics to seek ways of overcoming this problem, which is widely known as essentialism.

Essentialism and (mis)uses of strategic essentialism

When Hollinsworth tackles the problem of essentialism he argues that identifying an Aboriginal essence in terms of 'biological descent', for instance, can unintentionally lend itself to right wing populism, which creates a hierarchy of authenticity based on racist assumptions about categorisations such as full blood, half caste, and so on. This effectively derides some Aboriginal people with 'mixed ancestry' and lighter skin colour. He argues that there are similar problems of creating a hierarchy of authenticity with definitions of identity that situate an Aboriginal essence in terms

---

19 For a clear and astute study of negotiations of Aboriginal identity on talkback radio see S. Mickler, *The Myth of Privilege: Aboriginal Status, Media Visions, Public Ideas* (Fremantle: Fremantle Arts Press, 1998).

of 'cultural continuity' (cultural commonalities in terms of heritage, and ways of doing things). While Hollinsworth does show an awareness that the means of defining Aboriginality is seeped in Australia's racist history, he curiously acts as if it were possible to simply *choose* the most appropriate way for authenticating identity, by rejecting the above classifications for what he calls 'Aboriginality as resistance'. This latter category professedly describes an 'oppositional culture' to common experiences of dispossession and racism. Although he warns against the tendency to essentialise this 'discourse' of resistance, Hollinsworth contends that 'Aboriginality as resistance' is 'the most inclusive, dynamic and least readily domesticated by state co-option'.[20] Yet his choice to *settle* on a preferred category begs the question as to how such a selection can disentangle itself from its complicity with state co-option, as state co-option of identity *produces* such resistance and opposition in the first place. We will return to this issue later. For now, let us engage more specifically with the question of essentialism.

As already stated, this chapter is not intent on evaluating each of Hollinsworth's classifications. Instead its major concerns are to observe some of the ethico-political consequences of not interrogating protocols for speaking subjects within discourses of identity politics, and to point to what kinds of costs might be involved when we attempt to settle definitions of identity once and for all. Interestingly, in the *Oceania* debate, we can see that other authors question Hollinsworth's preferred classification, but they leave unquestioned the need to settle on a definition of identity *per se*. The problem of defining an identity always has and always will trouble the articulation of such an oppositional politics. The propensity for position taking around defining identities, exemplified in the logic of either/or arguments, often takes the form of debate between essentialism and social constructivism within identity movements. As seen in Hollinsworth's argument, he places definitions in terms of biology and cultural continuity on the side of essentialism. If the present chapter followed the same logic, we would place Foucault's archaeological analysis on the side of social constructivism. However, as Diana Fuss has noted, debates that rely upon taxonomic devices that oppose essentialism to constructivism are themselves 'overdetermined and constrained by the terms of the opposition in question.'[21]

Many proponents of identity politics handle the problem of essentialism by arguing for the use of a strategic essentialism. This phrase defends a notion of identity on professedly *political* grounds. Speaking about and for marginalised identities in the name of community building against systematic oppression, so the argument goes, requires the use of essentialist categories as an organising principle for subverting power relations. Unsurprisingly, one of the participants in the *Oceania* debate – Lattas – articulates such a position. He states:

> the way whites essentialise Aborigines cannot be rendered equivalent to the way Aborigines essentialise themselves for the simple reason that our ['white'] essentialism, which is part

---

20 Hollinsworth, 'Discourses on Aboriginality', p. 151.

21 D. Fuss, *Essentially Speaking: Feminism, Nature and Difference* (New York and London: Routledge, 1989), p. 1.

of a structure of domination, is not the same as the essentialism operating in a structure of resistance ... essentialism operates and means different things in different contexts.[22]

We can take for granted that constructions of identity materialise through relations of power, and the articulation of an essence will acquire different meanings depending on whether it is tied to structures of domination or to structures of resistance. The question remains, however, as to what precise political benefit strategic essentialism will proffer. The question is left begging as to how the categories of 'whites' and 'Aborigines' remain open to or closed from dealing with the exclusionary consequences of setting definitive criteria for marking authenticity. Are such categories, themselves, homogeneous and continuous unities? How does Lattas *account* for Hollinsworth's observation that there are Aboriginal people who articulate themselves as excluded or suppressed within prevalent categories of Aboriginality? Lattas's bid for strategic essentialism cannot account for the *specific* ways that express the diversity of Aboriginal identities. It seems that for Lattas, context is defined according to whether participants within certain discourses are 'white' or 'Aborigines'; he does little to indicate otherwise. Notwithstanding his own emphasis on context, Lattas gives the impression that the inscription of one's identity, and the relation one's identity has to knowledge, remain constant – if only strategically – no matter what the context. The criticisms levelled at Hollinsworth, therefore, fall short of acknowledging the materiality of discursive practices that inscribe *diversity among Aboriginal people*. Marcia Langton raises this point when she stresses the need to acknowledge cultural variation between Aboriginal people in terms of 'history, gender, sexual preference and so on'.[23] Correspondingly, it might not always be strategic to evoke an essentialist identity; sometimes identities might be crying out to be heard in their dispersion.

The dispersion of the speaking subject

So while it might be argued that presupposing a unity for a speaking subject, or a specific marker of identity, is strategically essential for effecting certain political transformations (a position that circulates within other orders of identity politics),[24] Foucault argues that it is crucial that such unities are not seen to develop as if they come into existence through their own accord:

---

22 Lattas, 'Wiping the Blood of Aboriginality', p. 162.

23 Langton, 'Well I Heard it on the Radio', p. 27.

24 The term 'strategic essentialism' is used not only within the confines of this particular debate, but has also been effected in other discourses, such as postcolonial studies and feminism. For example, see Spivak's comments on the Subaltern Studies group in her article, 'Subaltern Studies: Deconstructing Historiography', *Other Worlds: Essays in Cultural Politics* (New York and London: Routledge, 1987), pp. 197–221. See also, D. Fuss, *Essentially Speaking: Feminism, Nature and Difference*. For an account of the kinds of theoretical and practical ruts that can develop within discussions when essentialism is opposed to anti-essentialism, see G. Spivak and E. Rooney, 'In a Word: *Interview*', in G. Spivak, *Outside in the Teaching Machine* (New York and London: Routledge, 1993), pp. 1–23.

Should we regard them as illusions, illegitimate constructions, or ill-acquired results? Should we never make use of them, even as a temporary support, and never provide them with a definition? What we must do, in fact, is to tear away from them their virtual self-evidence, and to free the problems that they pose; to recognize that they are not the tranquil locus on the basis of which other questions (concerning their structure, coherence, systematicity, transformations) may be posed, but that they themselves pose a whole cluster of questions (What are they? How can they be defined or limited? What distinct types of laws can they obey? What articulation are they capable of? What sub-groups can they give rise to? What specific phenomena do they reveal in the field of discourse?). We must recognize that they may not, in the last resort, be what they seem at first sight. In short, that they require a theory, and that this theory cannot be constructed unless the *field* of the facts of discourse on the basis of which those facts are built up appears in its non-synthetic purity.[25]

An archaeological analysis deploys its 'negative work' (as Foucault terms it) by focusing primarily on the rules and procedures that come into play when specific issues are an object of enquiry: in this case, the status of the speaking subject, and the (dis)unity within the definition of an identity. As such, our major concern is to reflect upon the parameters in which the *Oceania* debate finds itself constituted. Rather than assessing the 'truth value' of claims made within the debate, archaeologies try to identify what factors must be at work for such claims to be assigned any truth value at all. By Foucault's account, it is only within the complex space of discourse that the rules for forming what is sayable, and what will count as legitimate knowledge, can be analysed. This space initially accepts 'the groupings that history suggests only to ... break them up and then to see whether they can be legitimately reformed; or [see] whether other groupings should be made'.[26]

Consequently, before an archaeological analysis considers the uses of strategic essentialisms against dominant discourses it is concerned with what rules and procedures identities *must* become complicit with when staking a claim that involves the identity in question. Here, context connects to institutional sites and specific discursive practices. This suggests that an identity that carries the same linguistic signifier from one context to another can still occupy a different signified in each of the contexts that effects its meaning. The discursive practices inhering in, for example, government bureaucracies, departments of Aboriginal Studies, newspaper articles, academic journals, talkback radio shows, community development programmes, school yards, and international conventions all adhere to their own sets of rules and procedures that *condition the space made available* for a subject to speak about that identity, *before* the speaking subject occupies that position concretely. Yet this does not mean that there is absolutely no regularity inhering in the same signifier of identity in all these spaces; on the contrary, identities as objects link to their own sets of discursive practices. For example, *before* any of Hollinsworth's students can *choose* a preferred way of identifying themselves, they are *compelled* to engage with the bureaucratic discursive practices of Centrelink (government department of social security in Australia) if they want to receive ABSTUDY (government sponsored

---

25 Foucault, *The Archaeology of Knowledge*, p. 26.
26 Ibid.

living allowance for indigenous students). This forces students to obtain a 'reference from an Aboriginal or Torres Strait Islander people's organisation which shows full details of [their] referee and length of time the referee has known [them]'. Verifying one's identity through an organisation and not one's own family might appear odd, if not insulting to many Aboriginal people. The matter is further complicated for many Aboriginal people whose Aboriginal heritage had been denied to them through the lasting effects of the Australian Government's policy of systematically and forcibly removing children from their families for over half of the last century.[27] Yet, students are positioned to situate their identity in this way for Centrelink's purposes. The very same students might otherwise identify themselves through biological descent, cultural continuity or resistance. They might identify through all three categories or none at all. But to be eligible for ABSTUDY their identity must be verified by an Aboriginal or Torres Strait Islander peoples' organisation. Hence, the institutional site of Centrelink governs students to articulate their identity in a specified discursive manner, even though their identities might be articulated differently in their own family and community contexts, when responding to media representations, or when engaged in political activism, and so on. In other words when various discursive practices intersect – as they do in the *Oceania* discussion – the object in question (Aboriginal identities) cannot be thought of as solely *outside of*, or *prior to*, the various discursive practices from which it acquires its meanings.

It therefore makes more political sense to situate differences between discursive sites in which Aboriginal identities are given meaning – the academy, the popular press, government policies, family and so on – than it is to reduce the meanings of identity to an assumed unitary (speaking or observed) subject. As Foucault explains:

> In the proposed analysis, instead of referring back to *the* synthesis or *the* unifying function of a subject, the various enunciative modalities manifest [the subject's] dispersion. To the various positions that he can occupy or be given when making a discourse. To the discontinuity of the planes from which he speaks. And if these planes are linked by a system of relations, this system is not established by the synthetic activity of a consciousness identical with itself, dumb and anterior to all speech, but by the specificity of a discursive practice.[28]

The specificity of the discursive practice is derived from the operational field of what Foucault calls the enunciative function (the place effecting any speaking subject that enters a particular discursive fellowship). Foucault further describes the discursive practice as 'a body of anonymous, historical rules, always determined in the time and space that have defined a given period, and for a given social, economic, geographical, or linguistic area, the conditions of operation of the enunciative function'.[29] *Without precluding the need to intervene in processes that produce*

---

27 See *Bringing Them Home: Report of the National Inquiry into the Separation of Aboriginal and Torres Strait Islander Children from Their Families* (Canberra: Commonwealth of Australia, 1997). This report is discussed in Chapter Four.

28 Foucault, *The Archaeology of Knowledge,* pp. 54–5.

29 Ibid., p. 117.

under-representation and marginalisation, an archaeological analysis suggests that when engaging with political struggles aimed at correcting discrimination and oppression inflicted upon marginalised identities, there is a need to account for the ways in which speaking positions and subject positions are *already effected* in an order of discourse. And this is one of the reasons why it becomes important to not group those inscribed with an Aboriginal identity in this debate as having an automatic ontological and epistemological standpoint for articulating a united front in politics, or univocal views of social reality, which can remain constant through all institutional sites and discursive practices. Yet, within the debate under discussion, there is a tendency to do so.

The function of Aboriginal identities in the *Oceania* debate

Of the six people participating in the *Oceania* debate, only one participant identifies with an Aboriginal identity – Mudrooroo Nyoongah.[30] According to the rules and procedures surrounding the rituals of speaking in the debate – although not unanimously claimed – Mudrooroo is situated with the most legitimate perspective from which to speak on such issues. That there is only one participant who speaks as an Aboriginal person in the debate is perhaps reflective of the rituals of exclusion mobilised by the rules and procedures surrounding academic discourses, a discursive space from which Aboriginal voices have no doubt been excluded and impeded (historically and institutionally) from entry. The lack of Aboriginal people speaking within academic discourses certainly needs redressing, but this issue cannot guarantee – and nor should it have to – that all Aboriginal people participating in such discourses would have a univocal perspective and unitary politics on issues of identities. The arguments for strategic essentialism, as well as Mudrooroo's argument for an Aboriginal essence, however, would seem to suggest otherwise. As Mudrooroo remarks,

> In this response, I have no wish to weight (European) theory against (European) theory, and then declare that this or that type of identity has more value; but see [sic] only to crystallize an Aboriginal (individual, though based on the views of many individuals and thus having a degree of commonality) response to the paper. It is thought provoking; but to suggest that an important Aboriginal theory of identity, an important social reality, may be weighed against European theories of identity, and then dismissed for being politically dangerous and a useful tool for racists seems almost pernicious, especially when for many Aborigines, Black, Brown, or Brindle, it is the Aboriginal 'essence' which makes an Aborigine and it is this essence which states, restates, informs and reforms his/her and our culture and social reality.[31]

---

30 As the writer in question has since dropped Nyoongah from his name, I will refer to him throughout in the main text as Mudrooroo. Mudrooroo has also been known as Colin Johnson, the name in which he is known as the first Aboriginal writer to publish a novel. He has also written under the name of Mudrooroo Narogin.

31 Nyoongah, 'Self-determining our Aboriginality', p. 157.

There is a certain danger involved in the positioning of the *enunciative-function* assigned to Mudrooroo – not Mudrooroo the concrete subject – from within the discursive practices effecting the debate. Because Mudrooroo speaks as an Aboriginal person, and can therefore fulfil the qualifications to speak legitimately within the debate, there is a danger that statements in his article might have the effect of quelling the diversity of other Aboriginal voices that might not share the same perspective. To take Mudrooroo's claim for an essence as self-evident because he is positioned with legitimate qualifications to speak makes it more difficult to give legitimacy to Hollinsworth's claim that *he hears* some Aboriginal people claiming they feel excluded from or repressed by current claims of what constitutes an Aboriginal essence.[32] A benefit in applying the negative work of an archaeological analysis to these issues in the debate is that we measure the question of essence by the way it functions in discourse, without committing to settle on a univocal and universal conception. For the problem with essentialism is not so much that an essence *per se* is invoked – there is no way around this as will be discussed in subsequent chapters – but that certain Aboriginal identities are suppressed or excluded from the kinds of essences that do currently circulate in attempts to define, once and for all, Aboriginal identity.

However, to complicate matters further with regard to the *Oceania* debate, shortly after its publication, it was reported in *The Weekend Australian* newspaper that an investigation had been underway for some time concerning the 'authenticity' of Mudrooroo's Aboriginal identity. The investigation was initiated by Dumbartung Aboriginal Corporation, 'a Perth-based organisation to promote and protect Aboriginal cultural activity'.[33] Like the *Oceania* debate itself, the newspaper articles concerning Mudrooroo's identity raises questions over authenticating Aboriginal identity. (It ought to be noted in passing, that apparently journalists are not as attached to the protocol of situating their knowledges by listing their identity markers in their writing – after all, their discursive practice of reporting the 'truth' is supposedly protected from personal partiality.) The journalist responsible for the reports, Victoria Laurie, quotes a definition of Aboriginal identity from the chairman of the Perth-based Aboriginal and Torres Strait Island Board of the Australia Council, Richard Walley. She also cites the concurrence of opinion held by the coordinator of Dumbartung, Robert Eggington, and the director, Lynette Narkle, of the Aboriginal youth theatre company, Yirra Yaakin: 'someone of Aboriginal descent who identifies as such and is recognised by their Aboriginal community to be so'. Laurie goes on to say that 'both Eggington and Walley are emphatic that "Aboriginal blood" is essential',[34] the definition that Hollinsworth rejects, but the grounds upon which Mudrooroo's

---

32 Hollinsworth situates his paper, 'Discourses on Aboriginality', as identifying different discourses of Aboriginality in order to analyse their 'implications for Aboriginal political struggles [and to] examine their consequences for urban Aborigines whose authenticity and claims to unique status in Australian political and cultural terrains are continually contested', p. 138.

33 V. Laurie, 'Blacks Question "Aboriginal" Writer', *The Weekend Australian*, 20–21 July (1996): 1, 12. This quotation, p. 1; V. Laurie, 'Identity Crisis', *Australian Magazine* in *The Weekend Australian*, 20–21 July (1996): 28–32.

34 Laurie, 'Identity Crisis', p. 32.

identity is contested. The concern over the status of Mudrooroo's identity, in the context of this chapter, cannot help but prompt the *Oceania* debate to confront certain complexities, *as* complexities and not as being resolvable in black and white terms, as it were. Such complexities are always at work when reducing speaking positions to the definition of an identity, regardless of whether the authentication of the bearer of that identity takes place.

If there are members of the Aboriginal community who advocate a definition of Aboriginal identity in terms of blood, and if these members of the community denounce the Aboriginal identity of Mudrooroo in such terms, then where does this leave the status of Mudrooroo's own identification or connections with Aboriginal experiences? Where does this leave his identity as an Aboriginal writer, a writer who remains on the curriculum of many courses in Aboriginal Studies in Australia? Mudrooroo's presence in curricula across Australia have engaged many Aboriginal and non-Aboriginal students alike in studies of Aboriginal literature. Many Aboriginal students have claimed that his texts resonate with their own life experiences.[35] Denouncing the authenticity of Mudrooroo's Aboriginality for many readers and critics engaging with this debate will also denounce his legitimacy in providing an Aboriginal speaking position that claims an Aboriginal essence. What happens to the status of those arguments that invest their own positions with recourse to Mudrooroo's authenticity? In effect *if* an argument is dependent on the authenticity of an identity and that identity turns out to be 'inauthentic' then *what critical leverage remains* to further political transformations? Even if no one disputed Mudrooroo's identity, what could guarantee one Aboriginal voice as representative of the diversity of others? Once again, Marcia Langton's point that the call for self-representation is often based on the 'assumption of an undifferentiated *Other*', is pertinent here.[36] We can now see that the matter of speaking calls for answers far more stratified and complex than a simple 'it does so (matter)/does not (matter)' alternative.

An archaeological analysis cannot provide definitive answers to the matter of speaking and claiming and contesting authenticity, but it does show that seeking definitive answers in the first place is misguided. Focusing on the rules and procedures that come into play when such questions are at issue rather than on markers of identity cannot relieve all anxieties about speaking positions, or make the matter irrelevant. But it can help to avoid conflating the legitimacy of a speaking position with a fixed definition of what constitutes an authentic identity for all circumstances and contexts. In stressing the importance of context, an archaeological analysis remains attentive to differences between those definitions of identity that circulate through the structures of bureaucratic authorities, through avenues of representation by proxy, and through different communities and media that articulate self-representation. Such an analysis is concerned with how all these differences might intersect or disperse within the same discursive formation.

---

35 See G. Lehman, 'Authentic and Essential: A Review of Anita M Heiss' Dhuuluu-Yala (To Talk Straight): Publishing Indigenous Literature', *Australian Humanities Review*, 33 (2004), accessed 28 December 2006, <http://www.lib.latrobe.edu.au/AHR/archive?Issue-August-2004/lehman.html>.

36 Langton, 'Well I Heard it on the Radio', p. 27.

To reiterate: when Foucault remarks that it matters little who's speaking, this is not to propose that subjugated voices should not be given more space to speak on their own behalf. Quite the contrary, as articulated in Foucault's discussion with Gilles Deleuze on the relations between intellectuals and power.[37] In intimating that it matters little who's speaking, Foucault turns specifically to accounting for the rules and procedures inhering in regimes of truth within specific contexts, which position what can be said, and who is deemed the most qualified to speak, *before* any speaking actually takes place. So with regard to the *Oceania* discussion, an archaeological study examines what regimes of truth are already in play, before a subject actually occupies a position that speaks about the construction of Aboriginal identities. If the voices of Aboriginal peoples are subjugated in the process, and if the marks of authenticity are contestable – as has become the case with Mudrooroo – the question needs to shift focus. We must then turn to what constraints on speaking already inscribe what is uttered; what constraints condition the authentication of an identity; and what possibilities are available for resurrecting the silence of its exclusions. Investigating such questions cannot avoid confronting the violence of the past. And here we return to the issue of complicity between discourses of resistance and discourses of power in the struggle over naming and contesting identity.

Tracing the violence of naming – 'Aboriginality' as a discursive formation

There is no doubt that narratives of (White) Australian history are riddled with the exclusion and suppression of Aboriginal voices; there is also no doubt that constructions of Aboriginality in Australia are saturated with the legacy of European invasion. Tracing the conception of Australian Aborigines in discourses of European colonial administrations clearly illustrates this:

> The concept 'the Aborigines' has been generally used as though such a self-consciously identified group had existed at first contact with Europeans, but this is to prescribe, retrospectively, a definition to the aboriginal peoples at a period when they had no such sense of themselves. Before 1788 or even much later, they did not conceive of themselves as 'Aborigines' any more than the European invaders thought of themselves as 'Australians'.[38]

The categorisation of 'Aborigines' in this way produces two related problems for current discourses concerning constructions of Aboriginal identities. First, such categorisation has had the effect of homogenising the diversity of peoples articulated

---

37 M. Foucault and G. Deleuze, 'Intellectuals and Power: A Conversation between M. Foucault and G. Deleuze', trans. D. F. Bouchard and S. Simon, in *Language, Counter Memory, Practice*, ed. D. F. Bouchard (New York: Cornell University Press, 1977), pp. 205–17. Within the course of this conversation, Deleuze commends Foucault for raising an 'absolutely fundamental' point concerning speaking positions – 'the indignity of speaking for others', p. 209. A critique concerning the issue of self-representation in this article is given in G. Spivak, 'Can the Subaltern Speak?', in G. Nelson and L. Grossberg (eds), *Marxism and the Interpretation of Culture*, (London: Macmillan, 1988), pp. 271–373.

38 Hollinsworth quoting Atwood, 'Discourses on Aboriginality', p. 138.

through indigenous regional terms such as Nyoongahs, Kooris, Wongis and Murris, to name a few – a point raised in a footnote by Hollinsworth,[39] and brought to attention by Mudrooroo in his article.[40] Second, colonisation forces these diverse voices to present themselves within Eurocentric discourses. On this point, Foucault's work on subjugated knowledges concurs with the political goal of wanting to trace the silences and exclusions of Aboriginal voices in the construction of their own identities.

Yet what overwhelmingly compromises the possibility of tracing the silences and exclusions of marginalised voices is the fact that the access to and articulation of such omissions from dominant discourses in the public sphere is inscribed through such dominant discourses themselves. Jacques Derrida raised this question with reference to Foucault's very early work, *Madness and Civilisation*, in his paper, 'Cogito and the History of Madness'.[41] Without submitting the details of the debate that ensued between Derrida and Foucault, it is sufficient to signal for now, and elaborate in later chapters, significant matters that impinge upon the present issue of authenticity in speaking positions.[42] For Derrida, Foucault's mission to retrieve the silenced and excluded voice of madness must presuppose an original *presence* for that voice – a voice that cannot not be caught in the web of metaphysics and what he calls the language of ontology. Put simply, in order to mark the origin of an historical exclusion from history, we are already participating within a web of signification. So violent acts in history, such as the British invasion of Aboriginal land, are inescapably complicit with what Derrida calls the founding violence of metaphysics – the space in which such acts acquire meaning. While this is not suggesting that events do not happen, it problematises the irreducible relationship between the event itself and the articulation of it.

Furthermore, for Derrida the assumption of an essence in the writing of such histories is 'a perilous necessity'. This is to say, while all attempts to settle on an essence might prove impossible, the very act of writing, as argued in the following chapter, cannot avoid presupposing such an essence. The political implications of this founding violence and presupposition of an essence are not immediately discernible, and are explored in more detail in following chapters. To mark the questions of metaphysical violence and the inescapability of essentialism here is simply to point out that there are further questions to put after an archaeological analysis. For now, however, it is equally important not to lose sight of the 'political' advantages of

---

39 Ibid., p. 152n2.

40 Nyoongah, 'Self-determining our Aboriginality', p. 156.

41 See J. Derrida, 'Cogito and the History of Madness', trans. A. Bass, in *Writing and Difference* (Chicago, IL: University of Chicago Press, 1978), pp. 31–63; and M. Foucault, *Madness and Civilisation: A History of Insanity in the Age of Reason*, trans. R. Howard (London: Routledge, 1967) [Fr. 1961]. Derrida's paper is the written-down version of a lecture he delivered at the Collège Philosophique in 1963, also published in this form in the *Revue de Métaphysique et de Morale*.

42 For detailed accounts of this debate, see N. Lucy, *Debating Derrida* (Carlton: Melbourne University Press, 1995), pp. 48–71; and B. Flynn, 'Derrida and Foucault: Madness and Writing', in H. Silverman (ed.), *Continental Philosophy II: Derrida and Deconstruction*, (New York and London: Routledge, 1989), pp. 201–18.

examining the speaking subject and subject (object) of enquiry, as functions of discourse.

As is clear from the rituals of speaking surrounding and infusing the *Oceania* discussion, there is an underlying imperative to situate the speaking subject's knowledges by referring to his or her own markers of identity. This particular rule of speaking is one of the regulating principles that operate within the *discursive formation* of identity politics in general and the politics of Aboriginal identities in particular. Foucault introduces the concept of the discursive formation to avoid referring to bodies of knowledges and practices 'as "science", "ideology", "theory", or "domain of objectivity"'.[43] The crucial difference between these organising concepts and the discursive formation is that the latter is more concerned with the '*system of dispersion*' effecting a particular object or thematic than it is with trying to link disparate events or smooth out contradictions inhering in their definitions.

> A discursive formation is not, therefore, an ideal, continuous, smooth text that runs beneath the multiplicity of contradictions, and resolves them in the calm unity of coherent thought; nor is it the surface in which, in a thousand different aspects, a contradiction is reflected that is always in retreat, but everywhere dominant. It is rather a space of multiple dissensions; a set of oppositions whose levels and roles must be described.[44]

Together the notions of discursive practice and discursive formation offer a means for situating Aboriginal identities in the order of discourse. Within the regulating principles of discursive practices that we have been examining, we can see how the enunciative-function attempts to ward off the materiality of discourse in an endeavour to master its chance events and to reconcile its disparities. That is, regardless of their intentions to accommodate diversity, all participants in the debate seemed fixed upon the notion of having to choose the most suitable 'discourse of Aboriginality', to borrow Hollinsworth's phrase. In doing so, they unwittingly quell the diversity inhering in Aboriginal identities and restrict the capacity for representations to shift in accordance with the specificity of a particular situation and institutional site. In other words, the status accorded to the speaking subject within the *Oceania* discussion becomes complicit in preserving the idea of a unitary sovereign subject, even though some participants, like Hollinsworth, might like to avoid this. Foucault is careful, however, not to completely diminish the creative role assigned to the enunciative-function. What he argues is that he has 'deprived the sovereignty of the subject of the exclusive and instantaneous right to it'.[45]

In contrast to the rarefying principles characteristic of discursive practices, the discursive formation is not intent on trying to define an object once and for all. We can therefore see Hollinsworth's search for the most politically effective definition of Aboriginality, for instance, as misguided from an archaeological perspective. Analysing the politics of identities as discursive formations would show that, no matter whom the speaker was, a specific identity could not be definitively pinned down in advance of the discourse in which it finds itself mobilised. In this sense,

---

43 Foucault, *The Archaeology of Knowledge*, p. 38.
44 Ibid., p. 155.
45 Ibid., p. 209.

Hollinsworth's bid to settle on a definition of Aboriginality as 'resistance' discounts the situations in which it might be more appropriate to speak of Aboriginality as 'descent' or Aboriginality as 'cultural continuity'. Equally, if Hollinsworth's critics had paid less attention to the speaking subject, and more attention to the rules and procedures that limit subjects when they speak in specific sites of struggle, the discussion could have moved toward a multiplication of strategies for intervening in various discourses and institutional sites where Aboriginality as an identity is at stake.

The arguments presented in this chapter demonstrate that it makes more sense to think about the question, 'What matter who's speaking?' in terms that first consider how a discursive space may effect an identity, before any speaking commences. Suspending reference to a speaking subject does not seek to absolve the investigator from responsibility, but instead enquires after what enables and constrains a subject in the very act of taking up a speaking position. As Foucault puts it in his own defence:

> If I suspended all reference to the speaking subject, it was not to discover laws of construction or forms that could be applied in the same way by all speaking subjects, nor was it to give voice to the great universal discourse that is common to all men at a particular period. On the contrary, my aim was to show what the differences consisted of, how it was possible for men, within the same discursive practice, to speak of different objects, to have contrary opinions, and to make contradictory choices; my aim was also another; in short, *I wanted not to exclude the problem of the subject, but to define the positions and functions that the subject could occupy in the diversity of discourse.*[46]

Suspending the status of the speaking subject is, however, only one strategy of reversal that Foucault deploys in his projects. The present chapter has been concerned primarily with this principle, because of its fundamental role in legitimising perspectives from which to speak within most of the discursive practices effecting a politics based on identity. This legitimacy is also entangled with the very nature of articulating an ontological standpoint from which some proponents of identity politics attempt to develop a new kind of scientific and historical objectivity based on the experiences of the subjugated. The next chapter looks more closely at the concept of experience, involving a discussion of how the terms post-postivist realism and postmodernism have come to represent different positions within a debate regarding the status of the concept. As both positions negotiate the question of origins, foundations and the constitution of identity positions for the purposes of furthering the aims of a 'progressive' politics, I argue that the generality in which such debates took form in the 1990s – and continues to have effects today – limits the possibilities for transformation. Such limits arise from failing to distinguish more carefully both the complicity and irreducibility between ontology and social criticism.

---

46 Ibid., p. 200, emphasis added.

Chapter Two

Between Experience and Epistemology

When Andrew Denton, host for the Australian talk show, *Enough Rope*, interviewed self-identified transvestite, Sara Lund (aka Claes Schmidt), from the 'Living Library Project' from Malmö, his first two questions were, 'How far back does the urge to express your femininity go?' and 'When did the word transvestite first come into your life?'[1] The first question asks for narration in terms of personal lived experience with reference to the memory of a certain desire. The second question looks for a link between this desire and a wider context from which to name this experience in terms of an identity. This latter question asks the interviewee to make sense of her *experience* in terms of social conventions and beliefs that are made available to her in order to classify herself as belonging to a collective identity (people alternated pronouns for Sara). Like many transvestites before her, Sara found an explanation for her desire to 'cross dress' – as it is traditionally called – in a book.[2] The word transvestite captured Sara's urge to express her femininity, but the book's entry also said that transvestites were homosexuals whose cross-dressing gave them sexual relief. My guess is the book was written prior to the early 1970s, when mainstream psychological and medical discourses made little distinction between transvestites, transsexuals and homosexuals, not to mention other forms of so-called gender and sexual 'perversions'. Sara had thought that she was heterosexual, and so was confused as to whether 'transvestite' was the appropriate word to describe her identity. The gap between Sara's personal lived experience with a conscious desire to express her femininity and her insertion into a tradition of naming that desire attaches to a fairly common feature in autobiographical narratives where genderqueer and non-heterosexual identities are at issue (although I am not sure that Sara would use the term genderqueer to describe herself). This feature uses a narrative constructed from the writer's own 'standpoint' of lived experiences to contest the legitimacy of official 'scientific' discourses of medicine and psychiatry that have subjugated their own identities as disorders and perversions. This chapter will draw out the

---

1   A. Denton, Enough Rope, ABC, 30/10/2006. Transcript available from http://www.abc.net.au/tv/enoughrope/transcripts/s1776670.htm.

2   The term 'cross-dressing' is seen as derogatory by some and as too constrained by prevailing gender binaries by others. As Riki Wilchins states, 'It's safe to say that nocross-dresser ever wore "women's clothes." If the bill came to him, they're his clothes, he bought them: They're obviously *men's clothes*. The displacement in naming them "women's clothes" prevents us from getting outside the terms of language, from getting to something new that might redefine skirts or dresses or femininity as being about men.' 'A Certain Kind of Freedom: Power and the Truth of Bodies – Four Essays on Gender', in J. Nestle, C. Howell and R. Wilchins (eds), *GENDERqUEER: Voices from Beyond the Sexual Binary* (Los Angeles and New York: Alyson Books, 2002), pp. 23–63. This quotation, p. 29.

distinction between the 'standpoint' of the lived experiences of a subjugated identity with different orders of making truth claims about that identity and knowledge in general. For as argued in the previous chapter, disentangling the matter of representing oneself from the idea that the subjugated speaking subject also occupies a privileged position from which to source the most legitimate truth claims is not always easy. To refine the distinction between lived experiences and knowledge claims based on that experience, I will engage with one of the most important and enduring debates on the concept of experience involving discourses of identity politics, which centres around the publication of Joan Scott's 'The Evidence of Experience'.[3]

Defining experience: between personal and collective identifications

Over the decades, we can witness a shift in genderqueer and queer autobiographical narratives as the places where the experience of finding a word to match the feelings for designating one's gender or sexual identity have become more accessible. Today a person can always do a Google search; the internet has opened the once tightly regulated discourses of sexuality, which were controlled by the church, the judiciary and psychiatric institutions. As so many personal narratives confirm, prior to the 1990s, when there was far less media and public exposure of non-normative sexualities and gender identities, knowledge about naming one's identity might have come from a chance reading of a magazine in a doctor's surgery or searching in a medical or psychological text for the closest word to match one's feelings.[4] The gap between personal first hand experience, and the available discourses that ascribe an identity to that experience demand that we identify relations between two kinds of knowledge. The first – lived experience – is subjective, while the second lays claim to a more public order of knowledge where some forms of knowledge have greater institutional legitimacy than do others. The relations between the two orders of knowledge – and for the moment we are only naming two – are not easily distinguishable. And this is why the concept of experience remains so contentious within discourses of identity politics. Before taking a closer look at relations between lived experience and categories available to explain and account for that experience as guaranteeing truth about identity, let's examine a few meanings for the concept of experience itself.

Experience

Experience occupies a privileged position in discourses of identity politics; this primacy together with the presumed self-evidence in which people use the term's

---

3   This essay was first published as 'The Evidence of Experience' in *Critical Inquiry* 1991. References here are from J. Scott, 'Experience', in J. Butler and J. Scott (eds), *Feminists Theorize The Political*, (New York: Routledge, 1992), pp. 22–40.

4   For a survey of autobiographical texts concerning various trans identities, including the 'pioneers' of transgenderism see P. Califia, *Sex Changes: The Politics of Transgenderism* (San Francisco, CA: Cleis Press, 1997). This book has since been updated (2003) since Pat has transitioned to Patrick.

meaning in everyday life, can go some way to explaining why debates about the importance of experience as a guarantor of truth continue to have currency. The term itself is not specific to identity politics, but has been subjected to interrogation and dispute over several centuries from many theoretical perspectives, including epistemology, history, politics, aesthetics and religion.[5] As Martin Jay notes, the word is very difficult to manage, since privileging one meaning over others, or seeking the origins of the word through etymology cannot settle all ambiguities and disputes. Nevertheless, some meanings are more useful than others are for clarifying current debates around identity, experience and knowledge. A particularly helpful distinction for sorting through debates about experience in identity politics comes from two German words – *Erlebnis* and *Erfahrung*, which are both translated as the one word, experience, in English. In her entry on 'Experience' (in a retrospective of Raymond Williams' famous, *Keywords*) Peggy Kamuf translates these words as follows: '*Erlebnis*, conscious lived experience of the individual and *Erfahrung*, experienced garnered from the past, including the past of a tradition into which the individual is unconsciously inserted'.[6] The first word, *Erlebnis*, readily lends itself to the lived experience that pertains to the first question Andrew Denton asked Sara concerning the urge to express her femininity. Jay adds to the sense of this word by stating that *Erlebnis* can refer to untheorised practices and can suggest a 'vital rupture in the fabric of quotidian life'.[7] There is also a corresponding relation between the word *Erfahrung* and Denton's second question, which was asked after finding the word to name Sara's desire/identity. For besides inserting an individual to a past of tradition, the word also suggests 'a more temporally elongated notion of experience based on a learning process, an integration of discrete moments of experience into a narrative whole or an adventure'.[8] This public and collective character of experience suggested in *Erfahrung* is relevant to aspects of identity politics, like consciousness-raising, where individuals are encouraged to reflect on their habitual and repetitious interpellations as particular forms of subjects (woman, lesbian, transsexual, etc.) that acquire a certain coherence. The emphasis within consciousness-raising in relating lived experience to power relations continues to inform identity movements' goals for social transformation. I will return to the distinction between *Erlebnis* and *Erfahrung* when discussing debate around Scott's critique of experience. In the meantime, it is important to note that I am ignoring other etymologies and meanings for experience in order to focus on the term's particular movements within discourses of identity politics.

The *OED* lists eight definitions for the term, providing Dominick La Capra with a base from which to explore connections between experience and identity through its disparate and conflicting meanings.[9] Several definitions comply with the concept of

---

5 See M. Jay, *Songs of Experience: Modern American and European Variations on a Universal Theme* (University of California Press, 2005).

6 P. Kamuf, 'Experience', *English Studies in Canada*, Dec. (2004): 3–4, Academic Research Library, pp. 24–9. This quotation, p. 28.

7 Jay, *Songs of Experience*, p. 11.

8 Ibid.

9 La Capra, 'Experience and Identity'.

experience currently effecting different identity based movements, where relations between 'knowledge' and 'actual observation' are constantly scrutinised. To cite only four definitions from the *OED*:

> the actual observation of facts or events, considered as a source of knowledge; the fact of being consciously the subject of a state or condition, or of being consciously affected by an event; the events that have taken place within the knowledge of an individual, a community, mankind at large, either during a particular period or generally. Knowledge resulting from actual observation or from what one has undergone.

These definitions certainly reinforce the notion that experience acts as an authorising principle from which to ground a shared unity between particular identities, while simultaneously functioning as a source knowledge. Such definitions circulate within identity movements in a way that is closer to the empiricist rather than metaphysical tradition in philosophy. For empiricists experience produces knowledge derived from the *senses* as opposed to innate *ideas*; we will call this opposition into question further down the track. It is now time to consider how these various definitions of experience impose themselves in debates about its status as a means for furthering social transformation.

The status of experience in identity movements

Debates about the place of experience converge on a number of questions that repeat themselves in singularly different situations – writing about women, homosexuality or victims and survivors of the Holocaust; whatever singular or plural identities might be at stake. These questions include the following. How does experience figure in constructing valid and reliable knowledge? How do the experiences of subjugated identities change the constitution of objectivity and prevailing standards of scholarship? What level of 'imaginative empathy' and re-enactment, if any, is possible for different investigating subjects dealing with the experiences of subjugated identities? How do different reading and writing publics handle exclusions and silences of subjugated voices in official records and textbooks of history? And how can both academics and activists refigure the very concept of experience in order to deal with perennial problems of the well-worn terms of essentialism and foundationalism? This last question often incorporates many of the others. For the status of essentialism and foundationalism was at the heart of the most impassioned debates during the 1990s, and both terms continue to haunt present reclamations of identity movements.

Discourses of identity politics are particularly sensitive to dealing with the problems of essentialism and foundationalism, even though there are recent claims that debates about these terms have 'died out' in some identity movements.[10]

---

10 See R. Halwani, 'Prolegomena to Any Future Metaphysics of Sexual Identity: Recasting the Essentialism and Social Consructionism Debate', in L. M. Alcoff, M. R. Hames-García, S. P. Mohanty and P. M. L. Moya (eds), *Identity Politics Reconsidered* (New York: Palgrave, 2006), pp. 209–27.

Despite the practical, political and philosophical impossibility of articulating a unified identity from which to base its emancipatory projects, identity movements continue to situate the problem of essences and foundations as something that they can overcome. One of the more enduring debates around this problem has its roots in how particular historians have responded to what has been described as the 'linguistic turn' in the humanities and social sciences, and finds its focal point of contention emerging from Joan Scott's widely cited and commented upon essay, 'The Evidence of Experience'.

Joan Scott delivered and published her paper on experience in an environment in which marginalised identities seeking to resurrect their lost voices in the dominant narratives of history had become prevalent. Scott identifies such 'corrective' writing in Samuel Delaney's autobiography, *The Motion of Light in Water*, where the latter reveals a cognitive dissonance between 'the prevailing representation of homosexuals in the 1950s as isolated perverts' and his *experience* of entering a bathhouse in 1963, which suggested a much more pervasive population of ('well adjusted') gay men. Scott describes Delaney's revelation in terms that readily fit identity based movements' aim to bring to visibility previously suppressed perspectives in the construction of reality – in this case, the construction of homosexuality. It also fits well with narratives of consciousness-raising, recently revived for critical analysis among post-positivist realists. But while such corrective accounts of history open the door to alternative perspectives that enlarge and challenge normative narratives in the history of sexuality, Scott argues that such evidence still accepts a referential account of history. For Scott, the concept of experience, as what one has lived through, becomes the origin of knowledge, which fails to account for the 'constructed' nature of experience. Scott claims that Delaney's approach renders experience as 'transparent' and does not challenge the ideological systems that presume a natural opposition between heterosexuality and homosexuality, sexual practices and sexual conventions. In order to challenge rather than reproduce the repressive mechanisms of ideology, Scott calls for attending to how historical processes are bound to discourses that *position* and *produce* a subject's experiences. While Scott does not explicitly define discourse, it appears that she is employing the term in the Foucauldian sense as described in the previous chapter. This alliance to Foucault is evident in Scott's conclusion, where she advocates the former's genealogical approach to history as the most productive way for the historian to relate the past – not by presuming the capacity to re-enact somebody's past experience, but through analysing changing concepts that make possible the 'evidence by which experience can be grasped'.[11]

Scott settles on this discursive approach after surveying various other historians' approaches to experience. What Scott finds problematic in the approaches of Raymond Williams, E. P Thompson and C. G. Collingwood is that they assume that experience is something that one 'has' rather than asking how the experiences of subjects themselves are produced. It might have been useful at this point to distinguish between personal lived experiences – *Erlebnis*, on the one hand – and *Erfahrung*, the traditions to which this subjugated identity have been inserted, on the other. For even if one concedes that experiences are 'produced' – which might

---

11 Scott, 'Experience', p. 37.

not be the most accurate way of describing one's insertion into the assignation of a collective identity – it is hard to remove the 'grammar of experience', to borrow Peggy Kamuf's phrase from a different context, which 'occur[s] most readily in clauses with the verb "to have"'.[12] This is perhaps why Scott's criticisms of previous accounts of experience were read as if the 'production' of experience discounted the ability to talk about one's own lived experience. This interpretation is captured in the bizarre title of Laura Downs's article, 'If "Woman" is Just an Empty Category, Then Why Am I Afraid to Walk Alone at Night? Identity Politics Meets the Postmodern Subject'.[13] Focusing on the title alone, we might wonder how Scott's call to analyse the 'substitution of one interpretation for another' in the history of the interplay between identity and experience could suggest that (any) identity is an empty category. On the contrary, it seems that Scott is indicating that interpretations of identity and experience are in fact rife with multiple and contradictory meanings. Moreover, to make any sense of Downs's title at all, we would have to presume a totally reducible relationship between the level of conceptuality (such as with the concept of woman) and the order of actuality (lived experience). As we will see, this chapter comes up against the impossibility of reducing the relationship between the ideality of a concept and the materiality of bodies to an essentialised and generalised form that can name a point of origin that privileges one order – either the material or the ideal – over the other. Scott does not appear to pursue this question, so I will leave it for now and return to her article.

Scott further argues that the aforementioned historians fail to put into question the foundational status of experience as a means for social transformation. Whether the historian is concerned with 'women or African-American or lesbian or homosexual [or] working class', the problem is the same.[14] This is to say, corrective history often equates personal experience with an automatic position from which to direct a politics of resistance. To give this criticism a wider context, I will outline its applicability to proponents of 'feminist standpoint theory', which despite undergoing several revisions over the last three decades, maintains the same basic premise – that the lived experiences of the subjugated are the best sources for constructing a socially transformative knowledge.[15] With its Marxist roots, standpoint theory began by extending the category of industrial labour – which invests the interests of oppressed workers with a privileged perspective from which to transform the world

---

12 P. Kamuf, *Book of Addresses* (Stanford, CA: Stanford University Press, 2005), p. 155.

13 L. Downs, 'If "Woman" is Just an Empty Category, Then Why Am I Afraid to Walk Alone at Night? Identity Politics Meets the Postmodern Subject', *Comparative Study of Society and History*, 35 (Apr. 1993): 414–37.

14 Scott, 'Experience', p. 30.

15 Feminist Standpoint Theory emerged in the early 1980s with Nancy Harstock's 'The Feminist Standoint: Developing the Guard for a Specifically Feminist Historical Materialism'. This article is now collected with a series of other essays on standpoint theory in S. Harding (ed.), *The Feminist Standpoint Reader: Intellectual and Political Controversies* (New York: Routledge, 2004). This collection also features Donna Haraway's 'postmodernist' critique of standpoint theory.

– to include the category of domestic labour, predominantly comprised of women.[16] Revisions of standpoint theory attempted to rectify previous feminist blindness to issues of race, and sexuality by attempting to add these perspectives of 'devalued and neglected lives' into a stronger concept of objectivity from that associated with the 'master position' (identified as white, capitalist and male).[17] Despite protests to the contrary, standpoint theory unwittingly implies that the subject with the most markers of oppression would occupy the most privileged perspective to construct objective knowledge (a black, third world lesbian with a disability, for instance). For Scott, such investments in privileging perspectives from the lived experiences of the subjugated obscures 'the contradictory and contested process by which [such categories were themselves] conceptualised and by which diverse kinds of subject positions were assigned, felt, contested, or embraced'.[18]

The most recent responses to Scott's critique, however, fixes on her treatment of John Toews and the status of relations between discourse, experience and truth.[19] Perhaps this is the case because Toews aims to rethink history's relation to meaning and experience in response to the so-called linguistic turn associated with the 'post-structuralist challenge to foundationalism'.[20] My aim here is not to adjudicate between Scott and Toews, as other critics have already offered detailed commentaries on both articles in question.[21] Rather, my concern is to chart how the

---

16 The crucial distinction between Marx's political economy and the neo-classical economics taught in most schools and universities today is that Marx accounts for the production of profit by analysing the extraction of surplus value that accrues by paying the labourer what s/he is worth as a *commodity* (the socially average necessary amount of labour to reproduce a labourer). Neo-classical economics advocates that the production of profit occurs in the sphere of *distribution* rather than *production* through the capitalist's skill and ability to reduce costs, take risks and seek new markets. Of course this is a very reductive account of the labour theory of value, but it is worth mentioning for this standpoint clearly distinguishes between a perspective that is linked to the production process as providing a perspective from which to understand *how profit accrues* and a perspective that is linked to viewing social reality more generally. This does not necessarily mean that labourers offer a superior perspective for grounding an epistemology, although there is a tendency for Marx and Marxists to suggest this as the case. For more detail on controversies over the labour theory of value, see E. K. Hunt, *History of Economic Thought: A Critical Perspective* (Wadsworth Publishing Company, California, 1979).

17 For Harding's most recent exposition of 'strong objectivity' see 'Transformation vs. Resistance Identity Projects: Epistemological Resources for Social Justice Movements', in *Identity Politics Reconsidered*, pp. 246–63.

18 Scott, 'Experience', p. 30.

19 J. Toews, 'Intellectual History after the Linguistic Turn: The Autonomy of Meaning and the Irreducibility of Experience', *American Historical Review*, 92 (1987): 879–907.

20 Scott, 'Experience', pp. 31–2.

21 Commentators on the debate include J. Zammito, 'Reading Experience: The Debate in Intellectual History among Scott, Toews and La Capra', in *Reclaiming Identity*, pp. 279–311; and W. Wilkerson, 'Is There Something You Need to Tell Me? Coming Out and the Ambiguity of Experience', in *Reclaiming Identity*, pp. 251–78; D. La Capra, 'Experience and Identity', and M. Jay, 'History and Experience: Dilthey, Collingwood, Scott and Ankersmit', in *Songs of Experience*, pp. 216–60.

proper name of Scott circulates as a postmodernist position from which other critics have allowed themselves to peg their own (op)position. As recent post-positivist realists concede that any subjugated 'standpoint' needs to acknowledge that 'all experience is mediated' through discourse and language, lived experience is still upheld as the starting point for constructing socially transformative knowledge. At the same time, some critics want to know exactly where experience is left as a source of knowledge if experience is *produced* through discourse. The matter is about to get quite complicated, not least because the very opposition between identity as a source of knowledge and identity as a product of discourse need to account for the *grounds* in which both claims are made. I will argue that both foundational and anti-foundational stances are not sufficient to deal with the status of experience. Consequently we will venture to a 'groundless ground' that is neither readily accommodated within Scott's discursive approach nor by her critics.

Experience and the question of origins and foundations

Not surprisingly, while vociferous critique followed Scott's paper on several fronts, the most lasting question for historians and those with investments in identity politics fixes on the foundational and epistemic status of experience. Wilkerson raises one of the more popularised problems that post-positivist realists have with 'postmodernism':

> If discursive practices actually produce our experience and identity, then the origin and reliability of my knowledge of these discursive practices becomes highly questionable. If my knowledge of these identity-and-experience-forming practices comes through experience, then it would seem that we are back to taking experience as the starting point for knowledge. This itself goes against Scott's basic thesis[.][22]

Such a criticism is akin to questions posed to Marx's materialism: if ideology is a product of our social material conditions of existence and this is what produces our consciousness, then how are we able to distinguish ideology from our real conditions of existence? Replace ideology with discourse and we have the same aporia. If we follow a Foucauldian response to Wilkerson's problem, as we would expect Scott to do, we would argue that a genealogical analysis bypasses the question of origins. For the genealogist's task is not to seek the *grounds* of a subject's knowledge, but rather to *track* the *dispersed manifestations* that position the subject as a function of various discursive practices and institutional sites that *produce* the illusion of a unitary subject. So rather than investing progressive politics and goals for social transformation with a truth that is grounded in experience through our 'real conditions of social existence', as Marx proposes, Foucault shifts the focus of examining knowledges and relations of power to what *counts* as true in such discourses.

Following this logic, we do not ask what truth *is*, or what a homosexual is, for instance, but ask what rules and procedures come into play in the construction of truth or the construction of homosexuality. Instead of looking for the permanence

---

22 Wilkerson, 'Is There Something You're not Telling Me?', p. 273.

of an object of enquiry (such as homosexuality) over space and time, Foucault is more concerned with charting the variability and transformations inflecting the same object through its constitution from various discourses such as law, religion, medicine, and psychiatry to name a few. Finally, instead of searching for the origins of an identity's authentic voice, Foucault follows Nietzsche's genealogical pursuits of 'cultivat[ing] the details and accidents that accompany every beginning'.[23] This is perhaps what Scott had in mind when calling for the substitution of one interpretation with another. Rather than emanating Delaney's 'revelation' as raising his consciousness, for this reinforces the idea of an authentic identity lying dormant within a subject, Scott prefers to consider different 'productions' of subjectivity made available by different networks of power/knowledge embedded in discursive practices. Foucault argues that such an approach evades the opposition between truth and ideology, an issue that according to Wilkerson leads Scott into 'irresolvable incoherence'.

For Wilkerson, maintaining the distinction between truth and ideology is crucial for shifting an identity's self-understanding from self-loathing to a raised consciousness of 'pride', as he claims is the case in relation to his own 'coming out' story regarding 'being' gay. He criticises Scott's reading of Delaney's experience for *not* stating why the substitution of one interpretation for another – from the isolation of feeling perverted to embracing an identity as part of a social movement – is *better* and more transformative. Claiming that 'Scott commits herself into a contradictory position', regarding how to explain Delaney's interpretative shift, Wilkerson states:

> On the one hand she continues to assume that there is something not captured by the categories available to Delaney, implying that his experience does have some meaning awaiting better interpretation; on the other, she claims that there is nothing beyond the available discursive structures to be understood, implying that there is nothing there but the production of discourses. So, on this postmodernist understanding, we seem to recognize that available understandings of the meaning of one's experience are inadequate while simultaneously implying that there is nothing in experience beyond the available understandings.[24]

Here, Wilkerson captures the most common response from proponents of identity politics to the infiltration of Foucault's genealogical analytics into their discursive fellowship. Wilkerson's conclusion about the so-called postmodernist attack on experience and identity is that by arguing that there is nothing outside discourse, critics like Scott undercut their own means of accountability from which to substantiate knowledge claims. Another version of this argument targets the oft-cited phrase from Derrida's *Of Grammatology*, '*il n'y a pas de hors-texte*' (there is no outside text; there is nothing outside of the text).[25] As we will see there is good reason not to conflate Derrida's work with Foucault's analytics of discourse,

---

23 M. Foucault, 'Nietzsche, Genealogy, History', trans. D. F. Boucahrd and S. Somin, in *The Foucault Reader*, ed., P. Rabinow (Harmondsworth: Penguin, 1984), pp. 76–100 [Fr. 1971]. This quotation, p. 80.

24 Wilkerson, p. 275.

25 J. Derrida, *Of Grammatology*, trans. G. Spivak (Baltimore and London: Johns Hopkins University Press, 1974), p. 158.

but for now the comparison allows us to isolate a common point of contention that trouble those who are troubled by the nebulous category of postmodernism and the purported idea that there is no outside to discourse or textuality. At issue lies the binary opposition of reality and representation (of an identity, for instance), which holds an analogous relationship to the opposition of materiality and ideality, the empirical and transcendental or in the terms of the present chapter, experience and epistemology. Before addressing this question of the 'outside', it is first worth extending Scott's problem with corrective narratives through a short detour of Foucault.

Scott's problem with Delaney, and by extension other accounts of identity that privilege revelations of raised consciousness, is that identity is articulated as if it existed *prior* to the discursive practices that produce the 'functional conditions' that make available the emergence, circulation and transformations of specific subject *positions*. This is certainly the way Wilkerson casts his own coming out story, as he refers to behavioural patterns and remarks from friends as signalling his gay identity as something 'already there', unnoticed by himself, but seemingly waiting to be uncovered. Wilkerson explains his new level of consciousness as emerging after recognising how he had internalised the ideological operations of homophobia, and so resisted embracing his own homosexuality. While this goes some way to explaining how various ideological state apparatuses interpellate experience, the revelation of 'accepting' one's gay identity maintains heterosexuality and homosexuality as a natural, discrete division and so cannot interrogate the presumed opposition of the division itself. We will come back to this. To follow Foucault's analytics of discourse, as Scott suggests, we need to shift focus away from a 'prior' identity in order to move toward those 'systems of formation' that provide the possibility for the constitution of an object or subject position as an identity. For Wilkerson, this leaves the subject too passive, constituted with no means of transforming an ideological version of identity to one that is more 'truthful', accurate and liberating.

Proponents of identity politics are not the only theorists to worry that such a conception of subjectivity undermines the subject's power to act.[26] But for Foucault, his analytics does not lead to a lack of agency or an inescapable trap within discourse on the part of the subject, as suggested by Wilkerson above. In identifying 'discourse as an ensemble of regulated practices' that constitute an object/subject, Foucault claims he also identifies the extent to which discourses 'can be objects of political practice' for subjects.[27] As many Foucauldian scholars commonly note, *the very same systems of formation that constrain* what can be said correctly about a given object – homosexuality, for instance – *also carry properties of enablement*. This focus on the *productivities* emerging from the rarefying procedures of discourse prompted prolific studies connected to the history of 'perverse' sexualities, whose focus was no longer compelled to rely on a pre-existing 'free' and 'natural' sexuality corrupted

---

26 See C. Norris, *The Truth About Postmodernism* (Oxford and Massachusetts: Blackwell, 1993).

27 M. Foucault, 'Politics and the Study of Discourse', trans. C. Gordon, in G. Burchell, C. Gordon and P. Miller (eds), *The Foucault Effect: Studies in Governmentality* (Chicago, IL: University of Chicago Press, 1991), pp. 53–72 [Fr. 1972]. This quotation, p. 69.

by social mores and constraints.[28] Notwithstanding the rebuttal of a natural sexuality, such studies at the same time seized upon Foucault's contention that 'homosexuality began to speak in its own behalf, to demand that its legitimacy or *'naturality'* be acknowledged, often *in the same vocabulary, using the same categories by which it was medically disqualified.'*[29] The possibility of articulating a reverse discourse, not innocent from the power/knowledge relations that produced that identity's constitution and subjugation, seemingly shifts the focus from retrieving lost voices for 'corrective' histories to charting the places of confrontation in which such subject positions exceeded available categories of normality and pathologisation.[30] To take Foucault's word for it, the obvious appeal of such an analysis professes not to presuppose an original unity to identity, but rather chart only the functional conditions that make available the space from which the fabrication of such an 'essence' emerges. Presumably, this approach does not grant foundational status to experience or a prior identity waiting to be uncovered, because it is not concerned with authenticating identity, but only the rules and procedures that govern what counts as true in an identity's articulation.

Critics like Wilkerson might object that a discursive approach to identity must still rely on the articulation of experience – however constituted or mediated – as a source of knowledge. For whether explained through ideological and repressive state apparatuses interpellating a subject, or through discourses producing various subject positions, post-positivist realists like Wilkerson maintain experience as a *starting point* for analysis to explain why some marginalised identities accept dominant narratives that produce self-loathing instead of the politically preferred oppositional consciousness. Once again the distinction between *Erlebnis* and *Erfahrung* would be useful here. For it is precisely this move from the personal experience that one 'has', to the political interpretation of that experience within a wider network into which one is unconsciously inscribed, which ought to prompt further questioning of the naturalised oppositional status between heterosexuality and homosexuality itself. Instead, heterosexuality and homosexuality remain accepted as intact identities; it is only the *hierarchy* of heterosexuality over homosexuality that seems to be in question for Wilkerson.

Although a seemingly unanswerable metaphysical question, asking after the origins and grounds of this division itself is not without political and ethical consequence. It is at this point in the analysis that both Wilkerson's post-positivist realist approach *and* Scott's Foucauldian discursive approach become complicit with what Derrida calls the metaphysics of presence. For it is at this point where having recourse to *either* a post-positivist realist account of experience *or* a discursive account of the construction of experience exhaust their capacity to account for the 'grounds' in which heterosexuality and homosexuality acquire oppositional status.

---

28 Books and articles influenced by Foucault's *History of Sexuality* are too numerous to name. For an incisive account that connects Foucault's works to activism see. D. Halperin, *Saint Foucault: Towards a Gay Hagiogrpahy* (Oxford: Oxford University Press, 1996).

29 M. Foucault, *The History of Sexuality: An Introduction*, trans. R. Hurley (Harmondsworth: Penguin, 1978) [Fr. 1976]. This quotation, p. 101.

30 See J.Terry, 'Theorizing Deviant Historiography', *differences*, 3,2 (1991): 55–74.

Both realist and discursive accounts reverse the hierarchy of privilege between heterosexuality and homosexuality, but they do not *displace* the oppositional logic that supports the hierarchy. The empirical recourse that both post-positivist realism and Foucault's genealogical approach to discourse share relies on a certain positivist acceptance of charting the appearance and circulation of categories (identities in this case) as a means to test reality. Neither approach considers sufficiently how the empirical articulation of an identity is actually dependent on what we will soon identify as a 'quasi-transcendental' structure to make any sense at all.

Experience and the founding violence of metaphysics

Raising the question of what limits both realist or Foucauldian accounts of experience is not to say that such frameworks are totally useless. That ought to be clear from the preceding discussion. For such focus on the subjugated identity of the pair can, to use Haraway's words, offer a 'visual clue' that something is not quite right in the grounding of ontology – of stating 'what is' – regarding sex, gender and sexuality.[31] That is, standing testimony to one's experience performs the crucial function of drawing attention to the oppressive frameworks and practices that inscribe identities differentially. We can apply this to Sara's experience in the opening of this chapter, for there is no biological or other reason, apart from what Judith Butler calls the regulation and repetition of gender norms that forbids a designated man from wearing a dress.[32] While post-positivist realists would start from Sara's experiences as a source of knowledge to reach a more objective construction of transvestite identity, a Foucauldian analysis would chart the functional rules and procedures that have made categories available to Sara from which she is constrained and enabled to name her identity. In an analogous way, realists would begin from the experiences of gays and lesbians to source knowledge about social transformation, while taking for granted gay and lesbian identity as something that is already there. In disputing this idea of prior existence, a Foucauldian analysis is interested in charting how homosexuality surfaces as a category of identity. In other words, post-positivist realists accept the categories of heterosexuality and homosexuality as given, while a discourse analysis looks for transformations of these categories without searching for a 'metaphysical' point of origin that gives rise to the opposition between heterosexuality and homosexuality. Even though Scott raises the question of the presumed naturalness of opposing heterosexuality to homosexuality, she does not pursue this line of questioning herself.

Had she done so in her interrogation of experience, the matter of writing corrective histories – or correcting any other disciplinary domain where identity based movements call for redressing previous exclusions – her interventions could have pushed debate beyond the false choices between essentialism and constructivism,

---

31 See D. Haraway, 'A Cyborg Manifesto: Science, Technology and Socialist Feminism in the Late Twentieth Century', in E. Weed (ed.), *Coming to Terms: Feminism, Theory and Politics* (New York and London: Routledge, 1989), pp. 173–204.

32 See J. Butler, *Gender Trouble Feminism and the Subversion of Identity* (New York: Routledge, 1990).

foundationalism and anti-foundationalism. The genealogical analytics that Scott follows can certainly mark 'accidental' beginnings for the naming of identities, as demonstrated in the case of Foucault's now famous observation that homosexuality did not acquire the status of a particular type of identity until the late nineteenth century.[33] For there is an obvious appeal for identity movements to mark the 'surfaces of emergence', the 'authorities of delimitation', and the 'grids of specification'[34] – the places, the authorities, and the classificatory rules and procedures that shape the formation of an identity as an object of inquiry – as this kind of analysis aligns itself easily to what we now call constructivism. But because the question of the relation between an inside and outside to discourse is not overtly addressed, Scott, like Foucault, talks herself into an anti-foundationalist stance rather than exploring further the necessity of accounting for the founding violence of (a) metaphysics (of presence).

Unfortunately, questions of metaphysics carry the burden of appearing to subordinate political questions to philosophical quibbles that seemingly have no bearing in the 'real world' of activism. So far, I have not considered the precise relations between philosophy and politics that allow such views to appear as common sense. Rather I have gone along with the presumption that we theorise experience in order to get a better account of identity for a transformative politics. I will put interrogating the common sense opposition between politics and philosophy on hold until I deal with the oppositional pair that provides the shared perspective from which Wilkerson and Scott think about the foundational status of experience: the opposition between heterosexuality and homosexuality. To recap: Scott wants to question the naturalness of the opposition by turning to how experience of one's sexuality is *produced* through discourse. Wilkerson wants to know how Scott can distinguish between truth and ideology, and side with more politically potent interpretations, in doing so. Following Foucault, Scott rejects the distinction between truth and ideology as insufficiently taking into account the relations of power imbricated in knowledge production. Focus on the rules and procedures for forming truth claims can tell us about how some knowledges become more legitimate than others and can alert us to how inclusions and exclusions are made in this process. Looking for transformations of the same object in its dispersal can show us that there is more than one meaning, often in contradiction to one another, for the same object. But can it show us that this same object is *never wholly one* in any of its manifest dispersions? And what is the significance of this disclosure?

It is at this point that Foucault (and Scott after him) assumes something like a full presence for an identity. For in tracking different dispersions of an identity, we only attend to the multiplicity of different manifestations of the presumed same identity marker. This *necessarily* presupposes identity as intact, or discrete. In other words, there is an *unavoidable essentialising moment* in any empirical historical investigation that must presume to know what it is looking for. This is where Derrida departs from Foucault, as he sees no escape from the metaphysical heritage that

---

33 Foucault, *History of Sexuality Vol 1*, p. 43.
34 Foucault, *The Archaeology of Knowledge*. These words, pp. 41–2.

permeates the order of intelligibility. To ask what renders something intelligible, we cannot not negotiate with metaphysics and the question of origins.

Contrary to what many critics expect of 'postmodernists', a category we ought to regard with utmost suspicion for effacing differences where we should note them, Derrida underscores the necessity of 'continuing to ask questions of origin'.[35] This is not to suggest that we will find a coherent answer to the question in the form of a simple, self-present and undifferentiated origin. On this point, there is an apparent alliance between Derrida and Foucault. For as we have seen through Foucault's genealogical methods, the search for origins reveals the contingency of accidents and events that 'produce' the (trans)formations of objects that acquire their regularity. But importantly for Derrida, the incapacity to trace a simple origin cannot evade the 'perilous necessity' of still pursuing the question of that origin, a pursuit necessary in giving an account for how such objects are rendered intelligible. Derrida demonstrates this point through an investigation of the history of writing and the writing of history, an investigation of paramount significance to the historical writings that mark the making of political identities:

> But the question of origin is at first confounded with the question of essence. It may just as well be said that it presupposes an onto-phenomenological question in the strict sense of that term. One must know *what* writing *is* in order to ask – knowing what one is talking about and what *the question is* – where and when writing begins. What is writing? How can it be identified? What certitude of essence must guide the empirical investigation? Guide it in principle, for it is a necessary fact that empirical investigation quickly activates reflexion upon essence.[36]

Not acknowledging the 'perilous necessity' of evoking an essence allows the study of identity politics as discourse to apparently escape from what Derrida would call the *founding violence* of metaphysics. For if the question of origins is confounded with the question of essence, as Derrida claims, then it makes no sense to take sides in the essentialist/constructivist or foundationalist/anti-foundationalist debate. In drawing attention to the *necessary presupposition of an essence* – the presupposition of what is – to the impossibility of ever securing that essence (what most proponents and critics of identity now both recognise), Derrida prompts us to think further about *what ties these contradictory positions together*. The issue therefore is *not* one of *overcoming essentialism*, but a question of how to work otherwise with the necessity of an impossible essence.

Experience and the ungrounded grounds of ontology

To return to the opposition between homosexuality and heterosexuality, we can see that an empirical investigation, in both realist and genealogical forms, can reveal what some critics call the 'contingent foundations' in which identities acquire their

35 Derrida, *Of Grammatology*, p. 74.
36 Ibid., p. 74–5.

meaning.[37] Both post-positivist realists and Foucauldian analytics can demonstrate how 'homosexual' *practices* have 'always existed' and both can track different institutional practices that have interpellated homosexuality as deviant. Both approaches can demonstrate and criticise the order of the hierarchy between heterosexuality and homosexuality here. But while the subjugated identity (homosexuality in this case) is measured against an opposite (heterosexuality) that requires such subjugation for its own self definition, political, ethical and philosophical critique can only go so far without questioning the grounds of the opposition itself. Because 'we know what we are looking for' in tracking the dispersion of the same object *we begin with a political position* that forecloses an openness to what might be calling for inclusion into that tradition. A critique of heterosexuality through the presumed opposite of homosexuality can easily remain blind to an interrogation of the binary norms that inscribe genders to bodies for identities, like Sara's, which do not readily fit these two available categories.[38] The question of a *non-oppositional otherness* inhering within the acquisition of meaning of hetero and homo sexual identities confines analysis to the logic of a binary grid without attending to the grid itself. But as with any oppositional pair, traces of other others call for reassessment of binary logic.

Questioning the binary pair of heterosexuality and homosexuality

As we have watched the signifier of homosexuality morph into the less exclusive but more unpronounceable acronym of LGBTIQ in the political arena, we get a sense that the binary grid of heterosexuality and homosexuality is bursting at its seams.[39] As historians have 'uncovered' categories such as lesbian, homosexual, gender and even man as relatively recent humanist entries in tracking how identities have come 'to be', we cannot be satisfied with a concept of identity as something that is already there. This seems to be Joan Scott's point in her analysis of Delaney. Scott wants to question the naturalness presumed between heterosexuality and homosexuality as oppositions, but her discursive analysis falls short of *displacing* this opposition. We

---

37 See E. Laclau and C. Mouffe, *Hegemony and Socialist Strategy: Towards a Radical Democratic Politics*, trans. W. Moore and P. Cammack (London, Verso, 1985); J. Butler, 'Contingent Foundations: Feminism and the Question of "Postmodernism"', in L. Nicholson, S. Benhabib, J. Butler, D. Cornell and N. Fraser (eds), *Feminist Contentions: A Philosophical Exchange* (New York and London: Routledge, 1995), pp. 35–57.

38 Apart from 'transvestites' disrupting the binary codes of gender and sexuality, there are also the categories of the intersexed and various trans identities. See S. J. Kessler, 'The Medical Construction of Gender: Case Management of Intersexed Infants', *Signs: Journal of Women in Culture and Society*, 16, 1 (1990): 3–26; S. Kessler and W. McKenna, 'Who put the "Trans" in Transgender? Gender Theory and Everyday Life', in S. la Font (ed.), *Constructing Sexualities: Readings in Sexuality, Gender and Culture* (Upper Saddle River, NJ: Prentice Hall, 2003), pp. 223–6; A. Fasuto-Sterling, 'The Five Sexes: Why Male and Female are not Enough', *Constructing Sexualities*, pp. 166–71. See selections also in anthology by S. Stryker and S. White (eds), *The Transgender Studies Reader* (New York and London: Routledge, 2006).

39 LGBTIQ in activist circles stands for lesbian, gay, bisexual, transgender, intersex and queer.

can attribute this failure to a lack of interrogation of the oppositional logic that she implicitly wants to question. If Scott had followed Derrida's interrogation of this logic, she would have had to confront the opposition between the empirical world and the 'quasi-transcendental' structures that render this world intelligible. While Foucault assigns a materiality to discourse, he remains unclear as to how discourse relates to ideality. In terms of identity, the opposition between the empirical and transcendental manifests as the relations between material bodies and identity categories articulated at the level of ideality. To speak of identities as *produced* through discourse, Scott leaves unremarked and unaccounted the idea that there is no outside to discourse – the question that Wilkerson claims leads her to irresolvable incoherence – when thinking through the relationship between the materiality and ideality of bodies. Judith Butler, co-editor with Joan Scott of *Feminists Theorize the Political*, attempts to tackle this very problem in her book, *Bodies That Matter*. The question of relations between the materiality and categorisation of the body arose after much confusion, criticism and acclaim for Butler's first book *Gender Trouble*. In *Bodies That Matter*, Butler asks:

> Is construction something which happens to a ready-made object, a pregiven thing, and does it happen *in degrees*? Or are we perhaps referring on both sides of the debate to an inevitable practice of signification, or demarcating and delimiting that to which we then 'refer,' such that our 'references' always presuppose – and often conceal – this prior delimitation? Indeed, to 'refer' naively or directly to the extra-discursive object will always require the prior delimitation of the extra-discursive. And insofar as the extra-discursive is delimited, it is formed by the very discourse from which it seeks to free itself. This delimitation, which often is enacted as an untheorized presupposition in any act of description, marks a boundary that includes and excludes, that decides, as it were, what will and will not be the stuff of the object to which we then refer. This marking off will have some normative force and, indeed, some violence, for it can construct only through erasing; it can bound a thing only through enforcing a certain criterion, a principle of selectivity.[40]

The problem Butler outlines here is one, which if taken further, will benefit from an overt engagement with Derrida's attention to the violence of metaphysics noted above.[41] For if we consider further the 'prior delimitation' that Butler invokes in

---

40 J. Butler, *Bodies That Matter: On the Discursive Limits of Sex* (New York: Routledge, 1993), p. 11.

41 Assessing relations between Butler and Derrida, however is quite complicated, as the place of the latter in the former's work can easily go unrecognised. Peggy Kamuf astutely remarks upon the curious place of Derrida in Butler's work in her essay, 'The Other Sexual Difference', *Book of Addresses*, p. 333n6. Kamuf notes that the 'relative absence' of Derrida in Butler's *Gender Trouble* appears 'as a more or less active effacement, rather than just a neutral non-appearance, since Butler does make use of recognizably Derridean terminology'. Kamuf illustrates her point by observing how in *Gender Trouble*, Butler uses the term *différance* in a way that is 'implicitly attributed to Irigaray and given an oddly restrictive sense'. We can extend Kamuf's observation to Butler's other texts. In 'Contingent Foundations', for instance, Butler refers to the Derridean terminology of 'non-originary origins' and 'ungrounded grounds' as shaping the effects of materiality that we come to regard as the foundations for our

the above passage, we inevitably find ourselves asking the types of questions that Derrida does when he questions the foundations of Western metaphysics at the very same time in which he acknowledges our indebtedness and ineluctable reliance on such thinking. This seemingly contradictory assertion provides a consistent thread throughout Derrida's works as he negotiates the status of presence and the ontological question of 'What is?' in various manifestations of the Western tradition, in philosophy, history and literature, among other domains.

When scrutinised within the zone of ontology, the concept of identity emerges as one that cannot be fully possessed, or be self present to itself – we cannot say that identity is this or that – even though we cannot help but presuppose such a presence. This presupposition of presence for identity (or any other concept for that matter) is an *effect* of a play of differential traces that inscribe the intelligibility of identity through the process of signification. The term Derrida uses to describe this general economy of signification is *différance,* though to prevent the term taking on transcendental significance Derrida deploys a series of analogous terms that always adjust themselves to the specificity and singularity of the situation or text in question. Such terms including writing, text, iterability, pharmakon, hauntology and autoimmunity are a few of the other terms Derrida deploys as *quasi*-transcendental structures that account for the legibility of all the oppositional pairs within the order signification. I refer to the general economy of *différance* here in order to prepare for more precise and specific operations of other quasi-transcendental structures in the following chapters. A brief description of *différance* here allows me to make the point that there is an *internal dissension* to meaning that makes it impossible to fully separate or completely collapse the materiality of lived experience from the ideality of the categories used to articulate that experience. As Caputo describes it, *différance,* 'precedes and contains all the oppositions that are inscribed within it'.[42] This would include the opposition between the material and ideal. Caputo appositely goes on to illustrate the differential play of traces in which 'our beliefs and practices' become '"inscribed"' by referring to the way in which we use a dictionary:

> The 'meaning' and 'reference' of a word in a dictionary is set in terms of *other words* with which it is internally related. A word has a 'place' in a dictionary, not only the one you have to 'look up,' which is a function of its graphic setting (its spelling), but also a semantic place or setting, a position, a range of connotation and denotation relative to other words (places) in the language. The meaning of a word is defined differentially, relative to the meaning of other words. What you will never find in the dictionary is a word that detaches itself from these *internal relationships* [emphasis added] and sends

---

negotiations between theory and social transformation with no apparent reference to Derrida. To draw attention to these matters is not to chastise Butler for being a neglectful scholar and neither is it to lay claim for propriety of Derrida over Irigaray. It is instead to consider how the direction of Butler's (re)negotiation with theorising materiality tends to obfuscate the significance of Derrida's critique of the metaphysics of presence for reconceptualising the very status of the political.

42 J. Caputo, *Deconstruction in a Nutshell: A Conversation with Jacques Derrida* (New York: Fordham University Press, 1997), p. 99.

you sailing right out of the dictionary into a mythical, mystical thing in itself "outside" of language, wistfully called the 'transcendental signified.'[43]

To put this in terms of the opposition between heterosexuality and homosexuality, *différance* marks a *preoriginary* space that makes possible the meaning of each term coming into being through their inscription within an internal 'play of differences'. At the same time, however, this condition of possibility for the acquisition of meaning is also a condition of impossibility for meaning to ever achieve a fully present, positive term. This internal division of meaning – without which we could not communicate or 'make sense' of anything – prevents any oppositional pair from being completely oppositional. In other words, oppositions are effects of the play of differences, where prior traces of these differences leave all oppositional predicates open to recoding. This priority of difference marks a non-originary origin rather than a simple origin – contingent or otherwise – as *différance* inscribes the very opening of history – the space from which empirical events acquire their intelligibility. *Différance* therefore does not mark an origin in terms of an historical moment. This non-orginary origin cannot be read as a 'rejection of foundationalism' as Wilkerson reads Derrida's critique of presence, on his way to criticising Scott. It is far more accurate to read *différance* as providing the space from within which the founding violence of inscribing any identity with the presupposition of an impossible presence takes place.

A new kind of experience

I have already noted how the opposition between heterosexuality and homosexuality has begun to give way by having to incorporate and name other differences within. As the LGBTIQ acronym suggests, the displacement of the aforementioned opposition has always been tenuous. But this is merely a sign that the grounds of the opposition are already shaky to begin with. There are transsexuals who identify as heterosexual and heterosexuals who identify their sexual practices as queer, both challenging the ability to be contained on either side of the binary. Transgender is now the umbrella term in which Sara's identity as a self-identified transvestite is supposed to fit. Yet, while Sara has adopted a female name, but is also known through the male name of Claes Schmidt. As a transvestite, Sara mostly mostly identifies as a man who likes to wear 'women's' clothing. Identifying as heterosexual, Sara remains in a relationship with the woman she married before she 'came out'. Sara does not fit on either side of the binary. The entanglements between sexual difference, gender identity and sexuality appear quite knotted, and are clearly not containable within binary logic. To stick with the example of Sara, as noted in an earlier footnote, Riki Wilchins underscores the limits of gender binaries by suggesting that cross-dressers are buying men's clothes (if the bill goes to him). In making this claim, Wilchins aims to bend the rules of gender norms against themselves.

> Many cross-dressers would reply that the point of dressing for them is that these *are* women's clothes. It is the otherness of the clothing, the fact that they are 'women's,' that is precisely

---

43 Ibid., p. 100.

what allows them to feel feminine. But once again, we can't get to someplace new, where femininity might be something about men that is not anchored in Woman (or vice versa).[44]

Derrida articulates a similar dream for something new – to open discussion of sexual difference, heterosexuality and homosexuality to something other than from within the confines of the binary grid.

What if we were to approach here (for one does not arrive at this as one would at a determined location) the area of a relationship to the other where the code of sexual marks would no longer be discriminating? The relationship would not be a-sexual, far from it, but would be sexual otherwise: beyond the binary difference that governs the decorum of all codes beyond the distinction masculine/feminine, beyond bisexuality, as well, beyond homosexuality and heterosexuality which comes to the same thing. As I dream of saving the chance that this question offers I would like to believe in the masses, this indeterminable number of blended voices, this mobile of non-identified sexual marks whose choreography can divide, multiply the body of each 'individual', whether he be classified as 'man' or as 'woman''' according to the criteria of usage. Of course, it is not impossible that a desire for sexuality without numbers can protect us, like a dream, from an implacable destiny which immures everything in the figure 2. And should this merciless closure arrest desire at the wall of opposition, we would struggle in vain: there will be never but two sexes, neither one more nor one less. … Does the dream itself not prove that what is dreamt of must be there in order for it to provide the dream?[45]

In the context of the above quotations, making sense of Sara's lived experience – as *Erlebnis* – also involves a confrontation with the traditions of binary gender normativity into which she is inserted – *Erfahrung*. There would be a place for Sara in both Wilchins's and Derrida's imagining of sexual difference and sexuality without numbers. This is not to negate the moments and sites of intervention that need to subscribe to the gender binary and logic of two. And nor is it to negate the personal, lived experiences of anyone. But while *Erlebnis* allows a person to say, 'this is what has happened to me', this person cannot be in full possession of that experience's entanglement with the otherness encountered in making sense of that experience as *Erfahrung*. This is not to say that an experience did not happen, or that experience is never relevant as a source of knowledge. It is rather to point out the limits within which making sense of one's experience necessarily occurs. For while one's lived experience is inserted into a more collective order of experience, the accumulation of experiences from which one supposedly gains wisdom is never one with itself. As Jay notes, 'experience, however we define it, cannot simply duplicate the prior reality of the one who undergoes it, leaving him or her precisely as before; something must be altered, something new must happen to make the term meaningful'.[46] Experience as an encounter with otherness leaves one open to the dream of experiencing the wall of opposition otherwise.

---

44 Wilchins, 'A Certain Kind of Freedom', p. 29.

45 See J. Derrida and C. McDonald, 'Choreographies', trans. C. McDonald, in *The Ear of the Other: Otobiography, Transference, Translation*, ed. C. McDonald (Lincoln and London: University of Nebraska Press, 1985), pp. 163–85 [1982].

46 Jay, *Songs of Experience*, p. 7.

A concluding note

Before leaving this chapter it is important to note that for experience to provide a source of knowledge for social transformation there must be a reckoning with the different sites of intervention and orders of analysis in which the experience of subjugated identities matter. Of course the lived experiences of subjugated identities matter as a source of knowledge when articulating equal opportunity policy, undertaking community based projects, or trying to redress previous exclusions from curriculum and canonical texts, although such articulations still take place within the space of a differential process of signification, for which there needs to be an accounting. Likewise, and as noted earlier, the perspectives of subjugated lives can help criticise certain institutionalised practices of power/knowledge relations by exceeding and challenging the existing norms and conventions that categorise identities in particular ways. But the lived experiences of the subjugated do not automatically provide a better source of knowledge than its predecessors for providing the grounds of a critical epistemology. For as Kamuf asked over thirty years ago, when speaking about feminist criticism, 'from where does it get its faith in the form of these questions [what is women's language, literature, style, or experience] to get at truth, if not from the same central store that supplies humanism with its faith in the universal truth of man?'[47] This is to say, the whole question of grounds is necessarily tied to a reckoning with its complicity with the language of ontology, which puts the whole presupposition of an intact identity that sources knowledge into question. Rather than lamenting the necessity of confronting the otherness into which one is inserted, the space of *différance* calls for working out and working through the play of differences and traces that have inscribed subjugated identities with a call for emancipation into a tradition which we have inherited. This heritage is not given to us, but asks to be read and translated from competing and sometimes incompatible codes and imperatives. By placing identity politics within a particular heritage of the emancipatory promise from which we must choose, the next chapter deals with the ontological limits in which identity movements order the realms of philosophy and politics in their calls for social transformation.

---

47 P. Kamuf, 'Replacing Feminist Criticism', in E. F. Keller and M. Hirsch (eds), *Conflicts in Feminism* (New York: Routledge, 1990), pp. 105–11 [1981]. This quotation, p. 108.

Chapter Three

Choosing One's Heritage:
Between philosophy and politics

Philosophers have interpreted the world in various ways; the point, however, is to change it.

(Karl Marx)

There is something about Karl Marx's Thesis XI that resounds as if it were the final word on defining the relationship between philosophy and politics. It captures the spirit of a promise for social transformation, which ostensibly gives philosophy its purpose. Given the current state of world affairs, the phrase still possesses a force that can readily subordinate the ontological question of 'what is?' to the presumably more pressing political question of 'what is to be done?' Yet, what at first sight looks like a deceptively simple imperative for ordering relations between philosophy and politics shows grave complexity and contradiction on closer inspection.

For discourses of identity politics, discourses inscribed by Thesis XI and slogans such as 'the personal is political', there is always the temptation to position philosophy and politics as inseparable from one another. From this point of view, every philosophy, every point of view and action, is political. The opposing view positions politics as completely separable from philosophy. From this position, one's political allegiances – even if sympathetic to the promise for emancipation elaborated in particular types of political philosophy – have nothing to do with philosophical reasoning or alliances with philosophical schools of thought.[1] As mirror opposites of one another, both positions fail to situate the two domains as interacting in what Gayatri Spivak calls a 'productive crisis'.[2] Of course, the matter of weighing up the precise connections between the two domains have a long history – both in the philosophy of ideas and the struggles and bloody wars in which politics is negotiated and fought. So to have any chance at seriously re-examining relations between philosophy and politics for identity movements, we must reckon with a certain heritage that has conditioned the articulation of these relations for the emancipatory promise 'today'. Derrida situates such a reckoning as a responsibility toward memory, memory that issues us with a 'sheaf of injunctions' from which we

---

1   G. Borradori identifies Hannah Arendt as belonging to the former position and Bertrand Russell to the latter in *Philosophy in a Time of Terror: Dialogues with Jurgen Habermas and Jacques Derrida* (Chicago, IL: University of Chicago Press, 2003). She identifies both Derrida and Habermas as two contemporary philosophers who are more akin to Arendt, but as we will see, such a positioning can be deceptive.

2   See G. Spivak, 'Can the Subaltern Speak?'.

must choose.[3] In the process of sorting through the heritage of injunctions, relations between the philosophical and political will not emerge as something that is reducible to a generalised, transcendental form. As we will see, to establish relations between the philosophical and political in advance, would be to forgo the chance of actually engaging with the *singularity* in which the emancipatory promise beckons us to countersign its future each time we hear its call.

This chapter responds to the call of a promise that is invested with a heritage that answers to connections and collisions between truth, liberty and reason in 'political philosophy'. The particular trajectory followed maintains a certain commitment to Enlightenment ideals that aim for some kind of squaring off between philosophy and politics. While I argue that such squaring off is impossible, this is not the same thing as capitulating to political paralysis. Such political paralysis has long been associated with 'postmodernist' thinkers by some 'left' intellectuals and proponents of identity politics. This chapter responds to the accusations of political impotence levelled at both Foucault and Derrida as postmodernists, and argues that the term postmodernism obfuscates differences between the two thinkers that ought to be highlighted. Foucault, for example, reworks Kant's Enlightenment questions, to consider what a progressive politics can make from philosophy, apparently without recourse to Truth and scientific reason. If we believe that we know what a progressive politics looks like, and if we are satisfied that we can clearly demarcate the limits of reason, Foucault offers a practical application of philosophy to politics – a path that many thinkers associated with the one the left have taken. However, for Derrida, reckoning with the status of reason and the relationship between truth and liberty is not a straightforward exercise that can readily establish a manifesto for a progressive politics. Instead of deeming Derrida impractical and useless for reworking Enlightenment ideals, however, I explore where attending to the radical disjunction between philosophy and politics might lead. The chapter therefore turns to Derrida's re-reading of both Kant and Marx as offering, to my knowledge, the most incisive re-evaluation of truth, liberty and reason for dealing with the 'productive crisis' between philosophy and politics 'today'. In order to reach this reading, however, we need to disentangle ourselves from debates about postmodernism.

The Enlightenment and postmodernism

The predominant form in which relations between the philosophical and political took place during the height of the 'theory wars', which swept through discourses of identity politics, centred around the status of postmodernism, particularly in relation to the Enlightenment.[4] Now of course both terms are invested with multiple meanings,

---

3   Derrida, 'Force of Law: The "Mystical Foundation of Authority'.

4   One of the earlier and most influential readings of casting 'postmodernism' as anti-Enlightenment is articulated in J. Habermas's, 'Modernity – An Incomplete Project', trans. S. Benhabib, in H. Foster (ed.), *Postmodern Culture* (London and Sydney: Pluto Press, 1983), pp. 3–15. In this article, Habermas chastises Derrida, Foucault and Lyotard for being anti-modernist and conservative. In the 1990s the presumed opposition between postmodernism and the Enlightenment became the central point of discussion for many conferences and

with the status of postmodernism's supposed departure from the Enlightenment becoming the focal point for countless books, journal articles, conferences and symposia from which to debate several key issues effecting the theoretical and practical considerations of movements concerned with social transformation.[5] Many of these debates situate postmodernism in opposition to the heritage of the Enlightenment, where the Enlightenment aligns with the modernist project of connecting the progress of knowledge based on reason to a *telos* of history. Twenty-first century proponents of identity politics continue to situate 'postmodernism' as repudiating the key concepts upon which such movements articulate their emancipatory goals, but there are also recent publications that renege on opposing the thought of those allegedly aligned to postmodernism to the Enlightenment project.[6] This chapter also does not oppose the two terms to one another, as the aim here is to follow a specific trajectory that connects identity movements to the heritage of the Enlightenment from Kant, through to the so-called postmodern thinkers that stand accused of breaking with the Enlightenment tradition. As stated, this line of enquiry will end by focusing on Derrida's reading of the emancipatory promise within Marxism, which provides the most prominent example of negotiating politics and philosophy on the world stage through the privileging a subjugated identity – the working class.

Peter Gay, a specialist historian of the Enlightenment, remarks: 'In its career as the target of polemical attack, the Enlightenment has been assailed for ideas it did not hold, and for consequences it did not intend and did not produce.'[7] The same could be said of postmodernism. For as the Enlightenment acquired the status of 'The Age of Reason' so postmodernism has become associated with an 'Age of Unreason'. Both labels have been misleadingly characterised as pertaining to a distinct period in history, the former as roughly spanning the years between 1689 and 1789 and the latter associated with our 'present' age. Unsurprisingly, such periodisation is highly disputed and now has the added complication that a 'postmodernist' stance rejects the totalising and teleological premises that such periodisation presumes.[8] Notwithstanding the sheer variety of different thinkers, the range of disciplinary objects, and plurality of cultural spheres associated with both of these terms, the Enlightenment and postmodernism have come to occupy convenient positions from which to situate presumed relations between philosophy and politics among other things.

When Jean-François Lyotard reported on the 'condition of knowledge in the most highly developed societies' to the government of Quebec, he defined

---

publications. To cite just one example among many, see L. S. Nicholson, S. Benhabib, J. Butler, D. Cornell and N. Fraser (eds), *Feminist Contentions: A Philosophical Exchange* (New York and London: Routledge, 1995).

5　For a more recent account of relations between postmodernism and the Enlightenment see K. M. Baker and P. H. Reill (eds), *What's Left of Enlightenment? A Postmodern Question* (Stanford, CA: Stanford University Press, 2001).

6　Borradori makes this claim in her introduction to *Philosophy in a Time of Terror*.

7　P. Gay, *The Party of Humanity: Studies in the French Enlightenment* (London: Weidenfeld and Nicolson, 1964), p. 262.

8　See J. Frow 'What Was Postmodernism?' (Sydney: Local Consumption Occasional Paper, no. 11, 1991).

the 'postmodern condition' as an 'incredulity toward metanarratives'.[9] For Lyotard, the delegitimation of a universal meta-language for arbitrating between scientific truth claims, and the breakdown in the grand narratives that tie progress in knowledge to a *telos* of history characterises the change from the postindustrial age to the postmodern era. He identifies two such meta-narratives as the 'dialectics of spirit' and the 'emancipation of the rational or working subject'.[10] Without entering into debates about the accuracy of periodisation and without interrogating a concept of the modern, to which the postmodern stands opposed, Lyotard's declaration on the state of knowledge marks a focal point in debates that gained so much currency regarding relations between the Enlightenment and postmodernism. This point concerns the status of reason as an arbitrator of knowledge and the extent to which there is a breakdown in connecting truth to liberty, progress to history and in terms of the present chapter, philosophy to politics.

'What is Enlightenment?' Reason, truth, liberty

It is the thread that connects philosophy to the world today that also interests Foucault in his essay, 'What is Enlightenment?', which offers a reflection on Immanuel Kant's essay of the same title, written two centuries earlier. Foucault wonders whether certain 'events' – such as the age marked as the Enlightenment – might be better approached by not restricting them to a calendar of universalised eras. He sees Kant's treatment of the same question as an instance in which philosophy's reflection upon its own present is examined as 'neither a world era to which one belongs, nor an event whose signs are perceived, nor the dawning of an accomplishment. ... He is looking for a difference: what difference does today introduce with respect to yesterday?'[11] What impresses Foucault in this sense of difference is the call to reflect upon how one's own philosophical enterprise might relate to contemporary reality: 'It is in the reflection on today as difference in history and as motive for a particular philosophical task that the novelty of this text appears to me to lie'.[12]

Interestingly, Foucault's turn to Kant prompts his own renegotiation with the status of Reason. While *Madness and Civilisation* engaged with the exclusionary effects of reason, Foucault's archaeological and genealogical works seem to avoid an overt engagement of reason, as he prioritised charting how truth claims *function* rather than how truth claims are *grounded*. But in reactivating certain aspects of Enlightenment values, Foucault finds an interest in Kant's distinction between the private use of reason and making public use of one's own reason. Kant introduces the distinction in his own essay when he defines the Enlightenment as '*man's emergence*

9　J.-F. Lyotard, *The Postmodern Condition: A Report on Knowledge*, trans. G. Bennington and B. Masumi (Minneapolis: University of Minnesota Press, 1984), p. xxiv.

10　Ibid., p. xxiii.

11　Foucault, 'What is Enlightenment?', trans. C. Porter, in *The Foucault Reader*, ed P. Rabinow (Harmondsworth: Penguin, 1984), pp. 32–50. This quotation, p. 34.

12　Ibid. p. 38.

from his self-incurred immaturity',[13] where immaturity is characterised by the 'lack of resolution and courage' to use one's own thinking without guidance from another. 'Immaturity' is characterised by accepting dogmas and formulas without question, which is to forfeit one's critical understanding that might otherwise be put to the service of the 'freedom to make *public use* of one's reason in all matters'.[14] As Kant states:

> by the public use of one's own reason I mean that use which anyone may make of it *as a man of learning* addressing the entire *reading public*. What I term the private use of reason is that which a person may make of it in a particular *civil* post or office with which he is entrusted.[15]

In making the distinction between private and public uses of reason, Kant distinguishes between a reason that is answerable to a higher authority – as with a clergyman who is under oath to preach a certain doctrine – and a reason whose freedom would be unlimited, and open to public question. That the clergyman is obliged to preach a certain doctrine as a civil servant, and might privately disagree with it, does not mean that the same clergyman cannot question that doctrine through public reason. The moment of Enlightenment would be when the latter type of reason – public reason – enables a type of government that would leave 'all men free to use their own reason in all matters of conscience'.[16]

The free use of reason for the Foucauldian subject

Foucault's interest in Kant's description of public reason lies in the idea that the free use of reason could potentially minimise institutional impositions placed on the ethical conduct of subjects. In pursuing the thought of 'today' as difference in history, Foucault's second volume in the *History of Sexuality* compares practices of self, through the control and governance of sexual behaviour, in modern Christian societies with those in ancient Greece.[17] His interest in the construction of the moral self in antiquity lies in contrasting the art of self-mastery with the contemporary practice of deciphering the truth about the self (as in the practices of confession and psychoanalysis) to expose the *non-necessity of basing ethics upon scientific knowledge of the self*.[18] Moreover, in order to attain self-mastery in the formation

---

13 I. Kant, 'An Answer to the Question: What is Enlightenment?', trans. H. B. Nisbet, in *Kant's Political Writings*, ed. H. Reiss (Cambridge: Cambridge University Press, 1970), pp. 54–60. This quotation, p. 54.

14 Ibid., p. 55.

15 Ibid.

16 Ibid., p. 59.

17 See Foucault, *The Use of Pleasure: Volume 2: The History of Sexuality*, trans. R. Hurley (New York: Vintage Books, 1985) [Fr. 1984].

18 The practice of self mastery is described in M. Foucault, *The Care of the Self: Volume 3: The History of Sexuality*, trans R. Hurley (Harmondsworth: Penguin, 1986). Foucault reflects on the non-necessity of basing an ethics on the truth of the subject in 'On the Genealogy of Ethics: An Overview of Work in Progress', in *The Foucault* Reader, pp. 340–72.

of the ethical self, the subject must employ the use of reason. And it is on this point that Foucault's 'ontology of the present'[19] finds connections with Kant's questions concerning Enlightenment:

> Kant in fact describes Enlightenment as the moment when humanity is going to put its own reason to use, without subjecting itself to any authority; now it is precisely at this moment that the critique is necessary, since its role is that of defining the conditions under which the use of reason is legitimate in order to determine what can be known, what must be done, and what may be hoped. Illegitimate uses of reason are what give rise to dogmatism and heteronomy, along with illusion; on the other hand, it is when the legitimate use of reason has been clearly defined in its principles that its autonomy can be assured.[20]

For some commentators, considering the conditions under which the use of reason is legitimate and the turn to the question of autonomy (for both reason and the subject) marks a welcome shift in Foucault's treatment of truth and agency. As Christopher Norris notes, the focus on how knowledges are invested with relations of power left Foucault 'no room for manoeuvre when it came to explaining how subjects could exercise a degree of ethical autonomy or choice, a margin of freedom that would not be foreclosed by the pervasive workings of power/knowledge'.[21] But as stated in the previous chapter, Foucault claims that his analytics of discourse is useful to a political practice insofar as discourse *can* become an object for political practice; this is to say, modes of subjection effecting a discoursing subject *limit* that subject's agency, which is not the same as negating agency altogether. Spivak succinctly describes this limit when reflecting on the difficulty of translating *pouvoir/ savoir* to power/knowledge: 'if the lines of making sense of something are laid down in a certain way, then you are able to do only those things with that something which are possible within and by the arrangement of those lines'.[22] This does not have to mean that subjects are determined by discourse through and through, nor does it have to mean that an agent's actions do not have effects beyond their intentions. According to Spivak, *pouvoir* implies a sense of '"can-do"-ness'. In other words, Foucault's notion of agency suggests that the ability to do something (or to intervene in a particular practice) is tied to the sense that one is able to make of it.

So while Foucault maintains an interest in the Enlightenment ideal that links the critical use of reason to liberty, he does not believe reason grounds either ethical judgements or political aspirations for liberty. This certainly breaks with a tradition that invests ethical and political conduct with the backing of philosophical reason and resonates with Lyotard's incredulity to meta-narratives. At the same time, however, Foucault maintains an attitude of reactivating the Kantian questions that James Bernauer rearticulates so well in Foucauldian terms:

---

19 See A. McHoul and W. Grace, *A Foucault Primer: Discourse, Power and the Subject* (Carlton: Melbourne University Press, 1993), p. 60.

20 Foucault, 'What is Enlightenment?', pp. 37–8.

21 Norris, *The Truth About Postmodernism*, p. 47.

22 G. Spivak, 'More on Power/Knowledge', in *Outside in the Teaching Machine* (New York and London: Routledge, 1993), pp. 25–51. This quotation, p. 34.

Foucaultian experiences of thought denature or historicize Kant's great questions. Not 'What can I know?,' but rather, 'How have my questions been produced? How has the path of my knowing been determined?' Not 'What ought I to do?,' but rather, 'How have I been situated to experience the real? Have exclusions operated in delineating the realm of obligation for me?' Not 'What may I hope for?,' but rather, 'What are the struggles in which I am engaged? How have the parameters for my aspirations been defined?'[23]

Foucault's turn of Kantian phrasing also turns the focus of identity politics away from questions such as 'Who Am I?' or '*What is* this or that identity?' to 'How have I been positioned to experience myself as a particular identity?' He is not looking for 'formal structures with universal value', but investigating 'the events that have led us to constitute ourselves and to recognize ourselves as subjects of what we are doing, thinking and saying'.[24] In situating his own archaeological and genealogical methods with such a critical attitude, Foucault sides with a certain Enlightenment value that he marks as 'the undefined work of freedom'. He declares that such methods therefore must be 'put to the test of … contemporary reality, both to grasp the points where change is possible and desirable, and to determine the precise form this change should take'.[25] Yet calculating what, where and how change ought to occur depends, in Foucault's terms, upon what sense is made of the relations between knowledge, politics and ethics. And it is precisely the way Foucault makes sense of what it means to put thought to the test of reality, or philosophy to the test of politics that allows him to *not* ask the question of what *grounds* these distinctions, or to ask what grounds the principle of reason. For as useful to a politics that the archaeological and genealogical rearticulation of Kant's questions might be, if the distinction between politics and philosophy remain uninterrogated and unaccounted for it is too easy to accept a certain dogma as to how philosophy, politics and ethics relate to one another. More significantly without accounting for what grounds the differences between philosophy and politics, the ordering of such distinctions become too readily answerable to a pre-determined concept of the political.

Answering for the principle of reason and choosing between injunctions

The difference Derrida introduces into reactivating the Kantian call for Enlightenment is one that takes responsibility for asking further not only what grounds the distinction between philosophy and politics, but also what grounds the principle of reason itself. For while reason institutes a principle of non-contradiction in adjudicating truth claims, the particular collisions between philosophy and politics in the articulation of the emancipatory promise are rife with seemingly irresolvable contradictions, which characterise the 'productive crisis' that Spivak identifies as essential for negotiating the disjunction between theory and practice. Rather than flee from the crisis where

---

23 J. Bernauer, 'Foucault's Ecstatic Thinking', in J. Bernauer and D. Rasmussen (eds), *The Final Foucault* (Cambridge, MA and London: MIT Press, 1988), pp. 45–82. This quotation, 46–7.

24 Foucault, 'What is Enlightenment', p. 46.

25 Ibid.

philosophy and politics contradict one another, this is where deconstruction's work begins. Before taking a more concrete look at these contradictions through what Derrida calls the various spectres of Marx, let's examine more closely Derrida's engagement with the Enlightenment faith in the principle of Reason.

When giving his inaugural lecture at Cornell University in 1983, Derrida approaches the question of reason, with reference to Kant in particular, by reflecting on the latter's assertion that the 'University should be governed by "an idea of reason",' and that speculative philosophy or pure reason ought to be kept separate from practical affairs.[26] This situates the 'University's reason for being' as having 'always been reason itself'. Of course such a positioning of reason leads to an 'unavoidable reflection' on ways in which university work is inextricably tied to the uses that might be made of it. If there was ever a time in which it was thought that the search for truth could be kept separate from 'any utilitarian purpose and to the orders of power' it is certainly evident now that such autonomy is impossible to maintain. And as Peggy Kamuf notes, it was only ten years after the publication of 'What is Enlightenment?' that Kant found himself reflecting on this very problem in the *Conflict of Faculties* after having confronted the issue of state censorship regarding the publication of *Religion Within the Limits of Reason Alone*.[27] There would hardly be disagreement from proponents of identity politics regarding the proposition that reason does not operate in the disinterested and neutral fashion upheld by the Enlightenment ideal. The entry of area studies such as Women's/Gender Studies, Minority Studies and the push for a more multicultural based curriculum in canonised knowledges from the 1970s onwards have all proffered interventions and critique of academic scholarship regarding patriarchal and monoculturalist bias in the University in particular and the operation of reason more generally. But as indicated in the previous chapter, to simply 'add and stir' oppressed markers of identity to a reason that evidently favours a white, masculinist bias still cannot ground ontology. It is not as if there is an outside to (white, bourgeois, masculinist) reason, to which marginalised identities can stand opposed. For, from where else would it be possible to articulate and make sense of a counter-position without at the same time being dependent upon and borrowing from the principle of reason that is supposedly being opposed? To try to institute an opposing stance would remain 'completely symmetrical to' the principle being brought into question and thus unable to deal with the crisis where the principle of non-contradiction reaches an aporia. I will come back to this principle of non-contradiction when examining the aporias within Marxism when the 'philosophical opposition' between materiality and ideality plays out against the 'political opposition' between communism and democracy. For now let's turn to Derrida's dual response-ability in answering *to* the principle of reason at the very same time as he answers *for* the principle by also questioning its grounding:

------

26 J. Derrida, 'The Principle of Reason: The University in the Eyes of its Pupils', trans. C. Porter and E. P. Morris, *Diacritics*, 13, 3 (1983): 3–20.

27 See P. Kamuf, *The Division of Literature*, pp. 135–6.

But to answer *for* the principle of reason (and thus for the university), to answer *for* this call, to raise questions about the origin or ground of this principle of foundation (*Der Satz vom Grund*), is not simply to obey it or to respond *in the face of* this principle. We do not listen in the same way when we are responding to a summons as when we are questioning its meaning, its origin, its possibility, its goal, its limits. Are we obeying the principle of reason when we ask what grounds this principle which is itself a principle of grounding? We are not – which does not mean that we are disobeying it either.[28]

Concurring with the Kantian call not to accept dogmas and formulas without question, Derrida takes responsibility for reason but at the same time does not absolve reason from scrutiny. Derrida departs from Kant insofar as he issues a responsibility that exceeds the conventional bounds of non-contradiction, calculability and the register of a seemingly neutral and unmodulated *tone* in argument.

In a different paper,[29] Derrida approaches this question of reason with a novel response to Kant's call elsewhere for adopting the appropriate methodological reason for resolving philosophical disputes and conflicts. In 'On a Newly Arisen Superior Tone Adopted in Philosophy' Kant opposes the trend that he observes in a 'superior tone' taken up by certain thinkers whose philosophical position professedly rests on intuition. He admonishes these thinkers for advocating that philosophical wisdom can emerge through 'listen[ing] to and enjoy[ing] the oracle within oneself' rather than undertaking the necessary work that accompanies the 'methodical development [of reason] and systematic arrangement of concepts'.[30] Furthermore, in having recourse to an interior voice for their wisdom, Kant claims that these pseudo-philosophers, referred to as the mystagogues, work against any progress toward developing a philosophical community. For Kant, philosophising 'under the influence of a higher feeling' will beckon philosophy's death, so seeking the proper tone from which to negotiate conflict in philosophy peacefully is of utmost importance.

While Kant favours a calm tone embodied in Reason, he delivers his response to the enthusiasts and mystagogues who listen to the oracle within with sarcasm and a somewhat mocking tone. In Derrida's reading, however, he notices that Kant is at the same time careful to leave room for a compromise with the enthusiasts.[31] Kant wants to reach a truce. After all, he is aligned to his adversaries insofar as he and they both want to speak and reveal the truth. So Kant offers a kind of peace treaty or contract to the mystagogues: not to personify the inner voice of moral law as some kind of veiled goddess, but rather to hear this law as the voice of reason. Kant supports his argument by claiming that 'the didactic procedure of bringing the moral law within

---

28 Ibid., p. 9.

29 J. Derrida, 'Of an Apocalyptic Tone Recently Adopted in Philosophy', trans. P. Fenves, in P. Fenves, *Raising the Tone of Philosophy: Late Essays by Immanuel Kant, Transformative Critique by Jacques Derrida* (Baltimore: Johns Hopkins University Press, 1993), pp. 117–71.

30 I. Kant, 'On a Newly Arisen Superior Tone in Philosophy', trans. P. Fenves, *Raising the Tone of Philosophy*, pp. 51–81. This quotation, pp. 52–3.

31 Derrida, 'Of an Apocalyptic Tone Recently Adopted in Philosophy', p. 142. Both Derrida and Fenves note that Kant is concerned with finding the correct procedures from which to conduct rational debate also in 'The Conflict of the Faculties'.

us into clear concepts according to a logical methodology is the only authentically *philosophical* one'.[32]

For Derrida, adhering to a logical methodology in answering to the principle of reason is only one part of the gesture toward responsibility for this principle. The other goes beyond the conceptual opposition of theory and practice, 'conception and application' philosophy and politics, or any other opposition for that matter. Importantly, however, one does not have to forgo one's professional competence, adherence to tradition or theoretical rigour to delve beyond the operations of conceptual oppositions that 'ground' the principle of reason. But, as Derrida convincingly suggests, for reasons that 'are more serious' than our own levels of (in)competence, clear and rigorous scholarship gets entangled with cryptic and shifting ontological foundations. Accounting for and working with shifting foundations takes negotiations between philosophy and politics beyond the realm of calculation to the risky order of an incalculable future for the Enlightenment's promise to ground liberty in reason. Derrida states:

> 'Thought' requires *both* the principle of reason *and* what is beyond the principle of reason, the *arkhe* and an-archy. Between the two, the difference of a breath or an accent, only the *enactment* of this 'thought' can decide. That decision is always risky, it always risks the worst. To claim to eliminate that risk by an institutional program is quite simply to erect a barricade against a future.[33]

In venturing to answer for the grounds of reason, Derrida does not shy away from the question of origins, even though such a venture moves toward an abyss, a bottomless ground that might 'risk the worst'. For it is precisely this question in which the *arkhe*, and an-archy governing what Derrida calls the metaphysics of presence conditions both the possibility and impossibility of propelling conceptual oppositions in motion in the 'first' place.

Derrida's reactivation of Kant's questions

The previous chapter ended by noting that Derrida's treatment of the question of origins is tied to his critique of Western metaphysics and its dependence on the presupposition of an original presence. An early interrogation of this presupposition was offered in Derrida's reading of *Madness and Civilisation* where he suggests that Foucault's marking of the Decision separating madness from reason is better thought of in terms of an *internal dissension* to meaning *in general*. This is to say, what appears as a division between conceptual oppositions can be accounted for in terms of a division that is 'interior to logos in general', thus disrupting the very idea of the division between exterior and interior.[34] This implies that there is a fissure at the origin of intelligibility, which binds the transcendental world of philosophy (and structures of thought) to the empirical world of politics (and historical 'events');

---

32 Kant, 'Of a Newly Arisen Superior Tone', p. 71.
33 Derrida, 'The University in the Eyes of its Pupils', p. 19.
34 Derrida, 'Cogito and the History of Madness', p. 38.

what, as noted in the previous chapter, Derrida calls a non-originary origin.[35] The radical intervention that the critique of presence offers is nothing less than a rethinking of the entire Western tradition. With regard to the thread followed in the present chapter, the critique of presence does not discount the Enlightenment ideal of connecting progress in knowledge to the liberation of humanity. But neither does such a critique attempt to maintain the emancipatory promise with a philosophical backup – an impossible task – or endeavour to adjudicate conflicts regarding the promise in terms that are solely reducible to reason.

Because Derrida does not align his own connections to the Enlightenment with recourse to a meta-narrative it is not hard to see how he can be grouped with thinkers such as Lyotard and Foucault. Yet because Derrida maintains that there is no escaping the metaphysical heritage in which philosophy and politics both acquire their meaning, and because this acquisition of meaning is accounted for in terms of an internal dissension of meaning in general, negotiating the heritage of the emancipatory promise becomes a far more active process in *choosing* between *contradictory* injunctions. This adds a further twist to the Foucauldian reworking of Kant's questions. While Foucault might turn the Kantian question of 'What can I know?' to 'How have my questions been produced?' there is still a certain transparency presumed in responding to the question. The register and structure of the question also situates the subject in a passive order of receiving a heritage as if it were discernibly decipherable. For Derrida responding to the heritage of metaphysics, and the Enlightenment along the way, involves a much more active and affirmative process. Further to the Foucauldian reordering of Kant's questions, I am also obliged to *sort through* the multiplicity of questions that beckon my response. From which questions do I choose? For it is not as if the 'different possibles' inhabiting the same injunction are readily readable. Thus the difficulty for Derrida in thinking 'today' in terms of the difference Foucault proposed through Kant involves a reckoning with a heritage that is not given. As Derrida puts it when responding to the heritage of Marxism:

> An inheritance is never gathered together, it is never one with itself. Its presumed unity, if there is one, can consist only in the injunction to reaffirm by choosing. 'One must' means one must filter, sift, criticize, one must sort out several different possibles that inhabit the same injunction. And inhabit it in a contradictory fashion around a secret. If the readability of a legacy were given, natural, transparent, univocal, if it did not call for and at the same time defy interpretation, we would never have anything to inherit from it.[36]

Derrida's re-reading of Marx will concretise the critique of presence for rethinking relations between philosophy and politics in terms that respond to the heritage of the emancipatory promise for identity movements 'today'.

---

35 Derrida's critique of presence based on this internal dissension of meaning appeared through the simultaneous publications of *Speech and Phenomena* (1967; Fr, 1973), *Of Grammatology* (1967; Fr, 1976) and *Writing and Difference* (1967; Fr, 1978; the book in which the 'Cogito' paper is reproduced).

36 J. Derrida, *Specters of Marx: The State of the Debt, the Work of Mourning, and the New International*, trans. P. Kamuf (New York and London: Routledge, 1994), p. 16.

The legacy of Marxism and the spectre of emancipatory promise

Current concerns with 'terrorism' disguise the fact that 'communism' was seen as the greatest threat to 'democracy' until relatively recently. This chapter asks, what *remains* to be thought of the so-called opposites between communism and democracy on the empirical world stage of history? Does the fact that 'democracy' has found a new enemy in (Islamic) terrorism mean that we are done with reckoning with the Marxian heritage associated with communism? It is worth considering this more slowly. Of course, the world stage has changed, but we can only dispense with the significance of Marx's vision for communism if we view its relationship to 'democracy' as mutually exclusive. Moreover, if we deem the relationship between communism and democracy as no longer relevant, we would have to assume that we can determine the ontological status of each of these signifiers – what communism *is* and what democracy *is* in actuality.

To focus on the struggle between 'communism' and 'democracy' is to reignite the heritage of the emancipatory promise in terms that evoke the *international* identity movement based on class. Such a focus calls for an accounting of the relationship between empirical events – such as the fall of the Berlin Wall in 1989 followed shortly after by the dissolution of the Soviet bloc – and transcendental ideals – such as that of communism and democracy. When Derrida responded to the call to deliver a lecture on the future of Marxism it was within the context of the so-called death of communism. Yet as Derrida notes in his address, and as many of 'us' identifying with the 'left' also experienced, a certain promise of communism had died long ago with its appropriation in the empirical world by totalitarian regimes.[37] In many ways, the dissolution of the communist bloc made it easier to speak more openly about re-evaluating Marxism. But how were 'we' to situate ourselves against the triumphant tone of the remaining superpower's claim that the correct path to humanity's emancipation had finally *arrived* under the banner of 'democracy' (in the form of free market capitalism) to the majority of the world?

An interrogation of the question of the *arrival* of the emancipatory promise, particularly as articulated in our Marxist heritage, can help advance a response. If there is complicity between Marx's communist ideal and the totalitarian regimes that appropriated this ideal, it is situated in the presumption of presence. In announcing that the *spectre* of communism was haunting Europe, Marx and Engels simultaneously called for the spectre to manifest. In other words, there was a call for the apparition to transform into actuality as the *arrival* of communism as event. Derrida questions the ability to presume the *presence* of such an arrival. For Marx, this presumption of presence became invested in transforming the material conditions of social existence, thus binding Marxism to chasing away all that is

---

37 There are a large number of thinkers who articulate such a position. See J. Derrida, 'Politics and Friendship: An Interview with Jacques Derrida', trans. Robert Harvey, in E. Ann Kaplan and Michael Sprinker (eds), *The Althusserian Legacy* (London and New York: Verso, 1993), pp. 182–231; Alain Badiou, 'Philosophy and the "Death of Communism"', *Infinite Thought: Truth and the Return of Philosophy*, trans., ed. Oliver Feltham and Justin Clemens (London and New York, Continuum, 2003); T. Eagleton, 'A Future for Socialism?' *Arena Journal*, 16, 1 (2000): 5–12.

deemed other to it: 'absence, non-presence, non-effectivity, inactuality, virtuality, or even the simulacrum in general'.[38]

Following Marx's struggles to rid the political once and for all from simulacra, phantoms, ghosts and spectres, Derrida examines the status of the spectre in *The Communist Manifesto, The Eighteenth Brumaire of Louis Bonaparte*, and *The German Ideology*.[39] The *Manifesto's* announcement that the spectre of communism was haunting Europe – not yet made present, but (almost) visible through the haunting possibility of its appearance – inspired fear in '[a]ll the powers of old Europe [who] ha[d] joined [*verbündet*] into a holy hunt [*zu einer heiligen Hetzagd*] against this spectre [*gegen dies Gespent*]'. This holy hunt evokes parallels with George Bush's 'coalition of the willing' – whose pursuit is devoted to expunging the threat of terrorism – insofar as there is a common axiomatic that ties the heritage of Marx's communism and totalitarian regimes of communism with present battles over the 'presence' of democracy in the world today. This axiomatic is invested in the conviction that democracy, like Marx's spectre of communism, can be incarnated as real presence, as actual living reality. The performative call to make manifest – through the formation of the communist party and international labour movement – what the Holy European Alliance feared as a haunting possibility, was a call to abolish the spectral status of communism: to convert the spectre to actual existence in the living present. But importantly, this fear of making the spectre manifest was not restricted to the Holy Alliance; Derrida demonstrates that 'fear before the ghost in general' is inscribed in the inheritance of Marx and the Marxists themselves.'

> To the ghost that communism represented for the capitalist (monarchist, imperial or republican) States of old Europe in general, came the response of a frightened and ruthless war and it was only in the course of this war that Leninism and then Stalinist totalitarianism were able to constitute themselves, harden themselves monstrously into their cadaverous rigor. But since Marxist ontology was also struggling against the ghost in general, in the name of living presence as material actuality, the whole 'Marxist' process of the totalitarian society was also responding to the same panic. We must, it seems to me, take such an hypothesis seriously.[40]

The lesson to learn from being caught within the panic of the ghost in general, Derrida warns, is that 'no one will ever be sure of being on a single and same side'. He adds, 'It is better to know that.'[41] It is not difficult to relate such uncertainty to the task of delineating a single and same side today regarding the meaning and incarnation of democracy.

---

38 Derrida, *Specters*, p. 39.

39 K. Marx and and F. Engels, 'Manifesto of the Communist Party', in *The Marx–Engels Reader*, ed. R. C. Tucker (New York: W. W. Norton, 1972), pp. 331–62 [G. 1848]; K. Marx, 'The Eighteenth Brumaire of Louis Bonaparte', in *The Marx–Engels Reader*, pp. 436–525. [1852]; K. Marx and F. Engels, 'The German Ideology', trans. C. Dutt, W. Lough and C. P. Magill, in *Collected Works, Vol. 5: Marx and Engels: 1845–1847* (London: Lawrence and Wishart, 1976), pp. 19–539 [G. 1845/1846].

40 Derrida, *Specters*, p. 105.

41 Ibid.

Between and beyond the material and ideal

For Derrida there is a certain spirit within Marxism that also remains within the Enlightenment ideal and beckons what he calls the democracy-to-come. Within his text on Marx, Derrida outlines this spirit as the call for interminable self-critique, the call for transformative interpretations of philosophy and the commitment to the emancipatory promise. But this spirit cannot be decontaminated from the several spectres that compete for its incarnation. Such spectres include the Marxists who argue for a pure form of Marxism that became corrupted by totalitarian regimes as well as those interpretations of Marxism upheld by totalitarian regimes themselves. Maintaining the spectres of Marx with a view to countersigning the emancipatory spirit within Marxism calls for an accounting of what renders readable all the different possible spectres around the same injunction. The issue for Derrida then becomes one of distinguishing the spirit of Marx from its many spectres. Such a distinction, however, remains undecidable as it is only through the many spectres of Marx that the spirit acquires its intelligibility. But rather than fleeing from this undecidable status for presumably being unable to provide a political programme for what is to be done, Derrida underscores the importance of reckoning with the passage of the undecidable as a call to responsibility. As Derrida notes elsewhere:

> A decision can only come into being in a space that exceeds the calculable program that would destroy all responsibility by transforming it into a programmable effect of determinate causes. There can be no moral or political responsibility without this trial and this passage by way of the undecidable. Even if a decision seems to take only a second and not be preceded by any deliberation, it is structured by this *experience and experiment of the undecidable*.[42]

And it is only by attending to Marx's negotiations with the undecidable status of the ghost in general that enables Derrida to rework the Marxist distinction between materiality and ideality for current re-negotiations of the emancipatory promise.

Recalling the famous Marxist axiom that it is being that determines consciousness and not consciousness that determines being, it is not difficult to see how dispensing with the phantasmogorisation of consciousness becomes an imperative for isolating the work to be done on practical, material structures of social existence. As many students of Marxism would know, the mere labelling of a philosopher as idealist – sometimes caricatured as being overly concerned with the realm of ideas and consciousness at the expense of real material structures – would often be taken as sufficient evidence for marking a philosopher's political impotence. But, as Derrida suggests, actual material conditions of existence *cannot be situated* other than with recourse to what he calls a 'quasi-transcendental' structure of ideality *without which the material structures in need of transformation could not be recognized as such.* Unfortunately, Derrida's recourse to such a quasi-transcendental structure, and his criticism of Marx's complicity with a metaphysics of presence, had prompted

---

42 J. Derrida, 'Afterword: Toward an Ethic of Discussion', *Limited Inc.*, ed. G. Graff (Evanston, IL: Northwestern University Press, 1988), pp. 111–60. This quotation, p. 116.

some commentators to accuse Derrida of fleeing from the call to political action.[43] Basically, such accusations rely on a tight opposition between the philosophical and political, where Derrida's attendance to the way in which the language of ontology binds all articulations of politics to the presumption of presence is taken as a mark of obstructing the path of 'getting on' with the real business of politics. Because Derrida does not offer a programmatic plan of contents that ontologises the promise, he stands accused of being overly philosophical at the expense of engaging with real world politics.

It is thus worth contemplating the status of the quasi-transcendental and the language of ontology in more detail than in the previous chapter. *For it is only by attending to such a space that the regulative tone of reason in philosophy can keep itself open to interruptions of the incalculable and urgent tone of the political, and the responsive tone of the ethical.* I will discuss the tension between the different tones of philosophy, politics and ethics in more detail in the following chapters. Such openness is essential in order to not collapse or render mutually exclusive all the oppositions that propel the progress of the promise's future. And it is this point that most often is missed by proponents of identity politics who try to come to terms with deconstruction.

The quasi-transcendental structure of the ghost, hauntology and spectrality

There is a sense in which the 'quasi-transcendental' operates on a level of generality, although as we will see later, deconstructive strategies aim to respond to what will be explained in the next chapter as the singularity of the Other. This level of generality relates to the minimal conditions necessary for rendering something (and nothing) as intelligible, readable or legible. Rodolphe Gasché refers to the articulation of these conditions in Derrida's work as infrastructures.[44] As outlined in the previous chapter, the best known infrastructure is *différance* – the neologism coined by Derrida whose difference to the French word *différence* can be detected only in written form, demanding that the usual hierarchy between prioritising speech (associated with presence of the subject) over writing (associated with absence of the subject) is disrupted. *Différance* questions the hierarchy implicit in such binaries as speech and writing and marks the general economy that exposes conceptual divisions as not fully determinate pure differences, but rather as always differential and deferred. Importantly, however, this general economy is related to a whole series of other 'infrastructures' which all mark both the conditions of possibility and impossibility for the presupposition of presence. Each evocation of a particular infrastructure – whether it is the supplement, iterability, writing, the pharmakon, among others – is specific to the text or problem at hand. As Derrida always painstakingly points out,

---

43 See K. Soper, 'The Limits of Hauntology', *Radical Philosophy*, 75 (1996): 26–31; T. Eagleton, 'Marxism Without Marxism', *Radical Philosophy*, 73 (1995): 35–7; Aijaz Ahmad, 'Reconciling Derrida: "Spectres of Marx" and Deconstructive Politics"', *New Left Review*, 208 (1994): 88–106.

44 R. Gasché, *The Tain of the Mirror: Derrida and the Philosophy of Reflection* (Cambridge, MA: Harvard University Press, 1988).

such conditions are not to be thought as 'general rules, applicable from the outside. A relative generality, strives each time to adjust itself to a text, a case, a problem, a singularity.'[45]

Each time an infrastructure is evoked to mark the quasi-transcendental, Derrida is concerned with an ineluctable presumption of presence that at one and the same time depend upon procuring an impossible point of origin for their existence. In the example of Marxism, the presumption of presence is manifest in the priority of the material over the ideal, the actual over the virtual, being over consciousness, the empirical over the transcendental, the concrete over the abstract, action over thought, and so on. Now as much as Marx might have wanted to maintain that these binary pairs stand in a dialectical relationship with one another that is in constant flux, the imperative to exorcise the German ideology of phenomenological Spirit bound him to the name of living presence as material actuality. That is, in order to uphold the thesis that material, actual structures of social existence need to be changed, Marxism becomes invested in chasing away all that renders the material intelligible and communicable (as belonging to the realm of the ideal). But this does not mean that such intelligibility can be explained by merely reversing the order of binary pairs so that the material is made subordinate to the ideal; the ideal does not exist in a vacuum. It acquires its form through its relation to the material world. What is taking place, then, is the inability to maintain these conceptual opposites (the material and ideal) as pure, equal and independent from one another.

This inability is equally pertinent in examining the operations of the opposition between the 'actual' and 'ideal' as articulated in the victorious tone of the so-called democratic super-power of the United States of America. On the one hand, the collapse of the communist bloc is upheld as signifying an *empirical, actual event* that democracy has finally *arrived*. But when we look to the empirical world to take account of how democracy measures up against its own ideal, we do not need to go very far to see that all is not going well in the capitalist nation states that have appropriated its name. As Derrida puts it, when 'chalking up to the account', when measured against the 'plagues' of unemployment, homelessness, economic wars between countries, and the unequal application of international law, amongst other things, the logic of the 'so-called empirical event' is discredited by the advocates announcing that democracy is here.[46] We can see that whether the emancipatory promise is situated in the ideals of Marxism or the ideal for a democratic future, we are troubled by the inability to say what the ideal actually is, or to be able to name its arrival. Yet this does not lead to abandoning the promise or the ideal. In reaching a point where oppositions – such as the material and ideal – cannot account for a simple point of origin for their existence, we inevitably reach certain limits of our thought. Far from leading to a relativistic dissolution of conceptual distinctions, Derrida calls for an-other logic:

---

45 Derrida and Sprinker, 'Politics and Friendship: An Interview with Jacques Derrida', p. 225.

46 Derrida, *Specters*, pp. 69, 81–4.

once the limits of phantasmogorization can no longer be controlled or fixed by the simple opposition of presence and absence, actuality and inactuality, sensuous and supersensible, another approach to differences must structure ('conceptually' and 'really') the field that has been reopened. Far from effacing differences and analytic determinations, this other logic calls for other concepts. One may hope it will allow for a more refined and more rigorous restructuration. It alone in any case can call for this constant restructuration, as elsewhere for the very progress of the critique.[47]

Derrida puts this other logic to work in *Specters* as the logic of the ghost, hauntology, or spectrality. Like the term *différance*, hauntology is a neologism invented by Derrida to mark an infrastructure within a text that makes possible the effects of presence without itself being given over to the present. In speech, the sound of hauntology is barely distinguishable from ontology; its difference is rendered intelligible in writing.

As the 'word' suggests, hauntology conjures up our relations to ghosts. Now while Derrida is not asking us to believe in ghosts as supernatural phenomena, he is asking us to acknowledge the *figure* of the ghost as that which disrupts our distinctions between the living and the dead, the actual and the inactual, being and non-being, and so on. In short, the ghost troubles the security of negotiating decisions – political, philosophical, or otherwise – in terms of the *living present*. This is to say the figure of the ghost forces us to deal with what Derrida calls the 'virtual space of spectrality': a space that can never be fully present to itself, which in turn does not mean that we are then marking a space of total absence.[48] That is presence and absence do not operate as simple opposites to one another within the logic of the ghost. This prompts us to think of the here and now as occurring within a time and space that is dis-adjusted with itself. As an apparition, the ghost is neither here nor there, neither then nor now, marking its absent presence in more *and* less than one place and time. Derrida meticulously draws out the implications of such a disjunction by offering a reflective reading of Shakespeare's *Hamlet*, in particular Hamlet's dilemma 'to be or not to be' in the face of an inherited responsibility. Hamlet's confrontation with the ghost of his father precipitates the judgement that 'The time is out of joint' and it becomes his responsibility, as his father's heir, to set things right. And just as Hamlet must deal with issues of inheritance, responsibility, and the promise for a future in response to the ghost of his father, Derrida claims that all of us living now – in this dis-adjusted time of the present – must deal with the question of inheritance, responsibility and the promise of a future in response to the ghost of Marx. This ghost also connects to the heritage of the Enlightenment.

And now that Derrida has joined those who are no longer here, it is up to us who are living to respond to the inheritance that Derrida leaves behind. As Derrida repeatedly reminds us that there are several spectres of Marx, and that these spectres cannot be gathered into one, we learn that an inheritance always involves interpretation, translation and choice, whether that relates to the Enlightenment or any of the identity movements discussed in this book. For Derrida, an inheritance – such as Marx's work, or the concept of democracy itself – is not merely given to

---

47 Derrida, *Specters*, p.163, emphasis added.
48 Ibid., p. 11.

us as some kind of transparent injunction. It involves work. It is a task of choosing how we negotiate the various spectres that attempt to *possess* a body of work, or indeed a task of reckoning with those spectres battling to possess the signifier of a particular identity. Derrida's negotiation of the spectres of Marx is also a negotiation with the spectres competing to embody the spirit of democracy today. For although the signifiers of communism and democracy were situated as opposite forms of governing nation states, the supposed opposing ideological positions to which they were tied – of the 'left' and the 'right' if one likes – both had their roots in the promise to emancipate humanity from all forms of oppression. This is to say, there can always be a 'left' and 'right' propelling the promise for emancipation, and there is always the risk of producing oppressive effects from the most well intended emancipatory goals. The *very same texts* (the *Bible*, Nietzsche's works, Heidegger's works, Marx's works) can give rise to *both* a progressive *and* a regressive politics. But how can 'we' negotiate these opposing possibilities such that the promise for a more just world does not get continually *possessed* by 'communities' (whether they are nation states, corporations, lobby groups, political parties, and so on) who appropriate the emancipatory promise to unjust ends?

It is the question of possession and appropriation of such terms as the Enlightenment, communism, democracy and identity movements such as feminism, to name a few signifiers associated with discourses of liberty, which continue to trouble how the emancipatory promise might be situated in relations between philosophy and politics. For whether concerned with the proper identity of social movements, such as communism, democracy or feminism, the proper identity for philosophy or politics, or the proper identity of woman, queer or communist there is no escaping the entanglements of otherness that 'establish' the groundless grounds in which each of these signifiers begin to distinguish itself. This is not to suggest that there are no identifiable oppressed subjects or that the content of what is happening in the world today under the banner of democracy is not of significance. And neither is it to suggest an abstinence from taking sides on such political issues, or in participating in political interventions concerning them. Such conclusions can be made only if the domains of politics and philosophy are reducible to one another.

Derrida's reading of Marx illustrates that philosophy and politics are neither separable nor inseparable from one another, which is quite different from rendering the terms mutually exclusive or collapsible to one another. This allows us to re-read Marx's Thesis XI in a way that remains faithful to the imperative to not merely interpret the world, but change it – yet in a way that maintains the irreducibility between thought and action. Put very simply, there is nothing stopping a person who philosophises about the promise for a democratic future from attending public protests, signing petitions, donating to aid agencies, voting as a citizen pariticipating in lobby groups, forming organisations that attempt to transform the powers that be and so on. What one chooses to do, however, cannot be decided in advance by an already prescribed political and philosophical programme that does not distinguish between the two domains. This is to say, at the heart of any claim to any kind of identity or philosophy or politics is an origin marked by difference and deferral, an otherness necessary to its acquisition of meaning. This mark of otherness also leaves open the possibility of appropriation to themes and circumstances unintended.

The consequences of taking this into account are not marginal. Without such an accounting, the domains of philosophy and politics are left with the illusion that their marks of propriety are self-contained – present to themselves. This stands for any oppositional pair. That philosophy and politics cannot be conceived as entities or realms that are comprehensible before the specific circumstances and contingencies in which they encounter one another is not at all a matter only for thematisation. It is also a matter for connecting philosophy and politics to ethics in the here and now.

As Derrida's reading of Marx demonstrates, in order to go beyond merely interpreting the world to transforming it, we must understand that what is happening 'now' always takes place in a *dislocated* present. I will expand on this dislocation of presence in the following chapter. Furthermore, and more importantly, we can no longer claim in good faith the ability to anticipate what the *presence* or *arrival* of an emancipated society would *be*. There can be no inheritance of the injunctions of Marx and equally no promise for justice without working with dis-adjustment – that is, working between 'two directions of absence, at the articulation of what is no longer and what is not yet'.[49] Thus plans for social transformation must account for this, and learn to work otherwise the very axiomatic of the metaphysics of presence, to which the (impossible) readability of such injunctions must remain bound. In the following chapter, I examine the question of how to connect such disjunction in terms of our response and relations with others. This takes us to the domain of ethics and the calls for justice.

---

49 This reference to working between two directions of absence is borrowed from Heidegger in relation to his reading of 'The Anaximander Fragment'. I will discuss this in more detail in the following chapter.

Chapter Four

Truth, Law and Justice:
Responding to the stolen generations
in the disadjusted time of the present

Paul is not the real name of the person whose story I am about to tell you. His anonymity is the condition upon which he tells his story – a story that will lead us to consider relations between law and justice – and appears in two very different publications. First, as testimony within the Report of the National Inquiry into the Separation of Aboriginal and Torres Strait Islander Children from their Families, entitled *Bringing Them Home*.[1] And second, as an expanded version in the anthology, *The Stolen Children: Their Stories*.[2] Paul's story appeared in *Bringing Them Home* as Confidential submission number 133. His opening sentence in both accounts reads, 'For eighteen years the State of Victoria referred to me as State Ward No 54321.' This number indubitably inscribes Paul's belief that he lacks an 'identity'; his proper name stripped to the debasing codes of state surveillance. In 1964, when Paul was five and a half months old, he and his mother became ill, and were both admitted to the Royal Children's Hospital in Melbourne. When Paul recovered, the Social Welfare Department of the hospital 'persuaded' his mother to 'board' him in St. Gabriel's Babies' Home. He reflects: 'If only Mum could've known the secret, deceitful agenda of the State welfare system that was about to be put in motion – eighteen years of forced separation between a loving mother and her son.' Before Paul had reached his first year, he was made a ward of the State. He cites the State's explanation: 'Mother is unable to provide adequate care for her son.'

Paul refers to the *Child Welfare Act 1958*, which allowed the County Court of Victoria to transfer him to Blackburn South Cottages in 1967 for '"suitable adoptive placement"' because they professedly could not locate his mother. There are grave doubts as to whether the authorities tried to find his mother, as Paul wonders why her address was not sought through the Aboriginal Welfare Board. As he later learnt, his mother's '[r]epeated requests about [his] whereabouts were rejected. All her cries for help fell on deaf ears by a Government who had stolen her son, and who had decided "they" [knew] what was best for this so-called part-Aboriginal boy.' Paul's first

---

1   *Bringing Them Home: Report of the National Inquiry into the Separation of Aboriginal and Torres Strait Islander Children from Their Families*. The full report can also be accessed through the Human Rights and Equal Opportunity Commission's website: http://www. humanrights.gov.au/social_justice/bth_report/report/index.html.

2   'Paul', in C. Bird (ed.), *The Stolen Generations: Their Stories* (Sydney: Random House, 1998), pp. 19–26. All quotations from Paul are cited from here.

placement for adoption lasted seven months. He quotes the Medical Officer's report that recorded that 'Mrs A "compared him unfavourably with her friends' children and finds his deficiencies an embarrassment, eg, at coffee parties".' (Poor Mrs A!) Paul was then placed in the Gables Orphanage in Kew, where he remained for two years. He recounts his feelings of 'being withdrawn and frightened, and remember[s] not talking to anyone for days on end'. He was taken to many homes on weekends during this time, but was always brought back to the orphanage.

Upon accessing his file through Freedom of Information, Paul learned that his 'dark complexion' posed a problem for prospective foster parents. Comments from his file emphasise that although he is 'part-Aboriginal', he could pass for Southern European, as Maltese, or Italian. Other comments stress that his colouring could be fully Caucasian, though his '"[n]ose and eyes could identify him as an Aboriginal"'. Paul was finally placed in a foster family when he was six years old, and stayed with this family until he was seventeen. He was never told about his Aboriginal heritage or his biological parents. He was the only foster child in the family who 'had four natural sons of their own'. His foster siblings would call him '"their little Abo"', underscoring Paul's already acute awareness and imposed shame of his skin colour. Throughout his school years, Paul was teased about his dark complexion, for looking different from his foster brothers and for not knowing his 'nationality'. He describes himself as having 'had no identity', and as being friendless and withdrawn.

Paul's foster family punished him severely, 'for the slightest thing they regarded as unacceptable or un-Christian like behaviour'. He 'would be locked in [his] room for hours' and 'wept uncontrollably' as he pleaded for his foster father to stop beating him with a leather strap. The beatings were countless. After refusing to give consent for his foster family to adopt him officially in 1981, Paul was kicked out of the house and told never to return.

Throughout their years of separation, Paul's birth mother relentlessly attempted to locate her son. State Welfare Authorities shelved all of the letters Paul's mother had written pleading for his return and withheld birthday and Christmas cards addressed to him. Upon his discharge as ward of the state, Paul received the entire collection of letters, cards and photographs as part of the 368 pages of his file. Only at this point was he told of his Aboriginal descent and that he had a 'Natural mother, father, three brothers and a sister, who were alive.' Upon release from the state, Paul's surname could change back to his mother's maiden name. The Welfare Officer gave Paul his mother's address, 'scribbled on a piece of paper … in case, in [the Officer's] words, "[he'd] ever want to meet her"'. According to the Department, all of this information was withheld for Paul's protection.

Paul recounts his reconciliation with his mother as instigating the most cherished years of his life. Sadly, his mother passed away after six years from their first meeting, 'at the tender age of forty-five'. Paul recites her parting words: '"I loved you then, and I love you now. Always believe that, my boy."' Mourning the loss of his mother, 'not once, but twice in a lifetime', Paul ponders his cherished years of reconciliation against the eighteen years 'snatched away from [them]'. He describes his relationship with his biological siblings and his aunts and uncles as 'fractious', feeling they are more like 'strangers', who have childhood memories he cannot share. With children of his own now, Paul 'cannot imagine the terrible, terrible trauma and pain [his] Mother was put through, for no reason other than the fact that she was Aboriginal'. In the anthology, Paul ends his story with a tribute to his mother in the form of a poem.

Reporting on the stolen generation

Paul's story is only one of over 1,500 stories submitted to the National Inquiry that records the personal accounts, policies and practices that were a part of the forced removal of Aboriginal and Torres Strait Islander children from their families and communities. Of these, 535 stories were transcribed from oral testimonies. Paul's story is singular; it cannot substitute for any other. His lived experience, like each experience recounted in other submissions, is unique. The report is filled with numerous stories and extracts from witnesses conveying the trauma of child separation; of physical, psychological and sexual abuse at the hands of those who were supposedly protecting them; and of the incomprehension of being taken away and forced to reject their ties to family, language and culture. It is impossible for Paul's story to encapsulate all others, and there is no theoretical, ethical or political justification for why Paul's story appears over others in this chapter. There is nothing extraordinary about Paul's story in comparison to others and it would be distasteful to say the least to build a hierarchy of trauma for the different kinds of experiences children went through upon separation from their families. Each unique story cannot be repeated here and the *singularity* of each story gathered under the auspices of the report spills over any attempt to collapse all accounts into an homogeneous whole. Yet, there is a certain pattern between Paul's story and thousands of others, whose numbers far exceed those recorded in the report; almost all of the children separated from their families were of 'mixed' descent, or 'half caste', to use the pejorative terminology of those times. Furthermore, without the generalising structure of the 'stolen generation' narrative, the hearing of each unique testimony would have easily remained beneath public audibility.[3] The tension between such singular stories and the necessary passage through the quasi-transcendental structures of intelligibility

---

3   The report was commissioned after a long process of lobbying by the Secretariat of National Aboriginal and Islander Child Care (SNAICC) and other activists. The narrative's coalescence emerged through the realisation that many Aboriginal and Torres Strait Islander children separated from their families had remarkably similar experiences and stories. For an account of how Aboriginal people connected their stories with one another on the way to realising that their stories were 'all the same', see L. Briskman, *The Black Grapevine: Aboriginal Activism and the Stolen Generations* (Sydney: Federation Press, 2003). Of course, the formation of the stolen generations narrative as *Erfharung* lends itself to members of the stolen generation to now recount their experiences (*Erlebnis*) with greater awareness of the traditions into which Aboriginal identity has been inserted. Bain Attwood makes a point of noting the difference between narratives concerning child removal before and after the stolen generations became the umbrella term from which to describe this experience. In doing so, he misses the significance of distinguishing between recounting one's lived experience and finally being able to articulate that expereince in a broader narrative, which up until very recently was 'officially' denied. See footnote 13 of this chapter.

necessary to register such 'incoming calls from the others', which shape the general narrative of the stolen generations, will guide this chapter.

As the Preface to the report stresses, the separation of Aboriginal and Torres Strait Islander Children from their families 'by compulsion, duress or undue influence is not an ordinary Report'. Sir Ronald Wilson, one of the two chief inquirers leading the Commission states that the usual determination of facts and conclusions aim to 'stand as an objective record, to be absorbed by the mind'. This report 'is spoken from the heart to the heart'. The report asks readers to *listen* 'with an open heart and mind' to stories that, unlike other national inquiries, were not required to 'prove' their experiences in a discourse of truth that would be accountable to a court of *law*. While the report investigates laws, practices and policies in Australia, the primary aim of the report is to give voice to those who suffered the impact of such separation. The report does not 'identify offenders for prosecution or as possible respondents to litigation. The objective is clearly not retribution, but understanding and healing.' We could say that the report answers to the call for *justice* as opposed to the rule of law.

Ethics, truth and ontology

Responding to the call of justice, as opposed to law, and prioritising the testimony as opening a space for a *hearing* of singular others over supplying a record of objective truth about the stolen generations shifts philosophical concerns from the language of ontology – where the question of 'what is' resides – to the ethical relation. The ethical relation, according to Levinas, *precedes all thematisation* of the self's awareness of its own being or consciousness, as it stands accused by the face of the Other,[4] in this case, Paul's story, as the face of the child separated from his mother. For Levinas, this relation is not to be confused with morality:

> By morality I mean a *series of rules* [emphasis added] relating to social behavior and civic duty. But while morality thus operates in the socio-political order of organizing and improving our human survival, it is ultimately founded on an ethical responsibility towards the other. As *prima philosophia*, ethics cannot itself legislate for society or produce rules of conduct whereby society might be revolutionized or transformed. It does not operate at the level of the manifesto or *call to order*; it is not *savoir vivre*. When I talk of ethics as a 'dis-interestedness', I do not mean that it is indifference; I simply mean that it is a form of vigilant passivity to the call of the other, which precedes our interest in being, our inter-est, as a being-in-the-world attached to property and appropriating what is other than itself to itself.[5]

---

4   In referring to the Other and other, I try to remain faithful to Alphonso Lingis's translation of *Le visage d'autrui* in Levinas's *Totality and Infinity*, trans. A. Lingis (Pittsburgh, PA: Duequesne University Press, 1969). Lingis states: 'With the author's permission, we are translating "*autrui*" (the personal Other, the You) by "Other," and "*autre*" by "other." In doing so, we regrettably sacrifice the possibility of reproducing the author's use of capital or small letters with both these terms in the French text' (pp. 24–5).

5   E. Levinas, 'Dialogue with Emmanuel Levinas', in R. Cohen (ed.), *Face to Face with Levinas* (New York: State University of New York Press, 1986), pp. 13–33. This quotation, p. 29.

This concern with 'appropriating what is other than itself to itself' is one way of describing the British colonisation of Aboriginal Australia, a point to which we will return as a necessary backdrop to the stolen generations narrative. This narrative also calls for a reading against current debates concerning 'Reconciliation' – the professedly unifying movement toward healing the wounds of past injustices toward Australia's Aboriginal people. Taking this turn of situating stories from the stolen generations and the call for reconciliation within the highly abstract terminology of Levinas's concern with the ethical relation, however, might at first sight appear excessive to discourses of identity politics. Yet, here, in the context of examining identity politics in deconstruction, highlighting both the *irreducibility and indissociability* between the realms of ontology, politics and ethics can offer a way of rethinking relations between truth, law and justice, as they are currently obfuscated in the 'history wars' about the stolen generations.[6] For shifting the language of ontology to the ethical relation and from the site of 'truth' to justice, is not through a simple disregard for truth. Ordering relations between truth, law and justice in coming to terms with the thought of appropriating what is other to a self requires a more complex detour through the language of ontology. For as Derrida argues, negotiating the shift from ontology to the ethical relation can produce the very form of violence toward the other that Levinas seeks to overcome if we follow Levinas's view that the other's relation to self is considered absolute. To recognise the significance of this, it is necessary to situate the ontological status of the other in more detail.

The issue of violence toward the other turns on the extent to which the other can be conceived in terms of an *absolute* alterity. To put this in concrete terms of the present discussion it would be to argue that Aboriginal people are absolutely other to the British colonists. The face of the Other is non-subsumable, implying that any attempt to reduce the Other to the same would be an act of violence. But if the ethical relation precedes all thematisation (situating ethics as prior to the ontological question of 'what is') and cannot be reduced to the language of the same, as Levinas maintains, Derrida asks, how is it possible to state this without first submitting to the language of ontology? To put this another way, if the alterity of the other is

---

6   In Australia, the history wars centre on the appropriateness of naming the founding (physical) violence that robbed sovereignty from Aboriginal peoples already living on this land. Frontier violence included massacres as well as the separation of Aboriginal children from their families, communities, language and cultural traditions discussed in this chapter. History wars rose to fever pitch with the publication of Keith Windschuttle's *The Fabrication of Aboriginal History*. Bain Attwood notes that both national and international media accumulated around one hundred articles, more than one hundred letters to the editors in the press, and significant television and radio coverage in the first year after the book's publication alone. Public debates proliferated, taking place most notably in the Australian conservative magazine, *The Quadrant*, well known as a favourite read for Australia's former Prime Minister, John Howard. The history wars have not only raised questions about 'objectivity' in history and the place of experience in documenting past events, but raises the issue of how all citizens might engage with the bleeding of boundaries between media coverage, academic investigation and government policy.

absolute, how am I able to recognise and form a *relation* to the Other?[7] Would a perception of absolute alterity succumb to a violence that a relational alterity better resists? Following Husserl, Derrida states the importance of recognising that the irreducibility of the Other to an ego (my ego) is accompanied by conceding that in order to respect this irreducibility and alterity of the other there must be a certain phenomenon of the other as alter ego. In other words, 'the other as transcendental other … can never be given to me in an original way and in person, but only through analogical appresentation'.[8] On this account, the other cannot be reduced to the same, because it is impossible for the same to be able to see from the perspective of the other; the 'other as alter ego signifies the other as other, irreducible to *my* ego, precisely because it is an ego, because it has the form of the ego'.[9] With the recognition of this economy comes the recognition that every self is also the other's other. Without the recognition of this economy 'I could not desire (or) respect the other in ethical dissymmetry'.[10] Derrida therefore refers to this recognition as 'evidence of a strange symmetry'.[11] This is to say, in order to speak of the Other, without robbing oneself of the means to do so, there must be a negotiation with a transcendental violence – a language that speaks to the other in the economy of the same – which renders the other intelligible. As Drucilla Cornell puts it, 'Without this moment of universality the otherness of the Other can be only too easily reduced to mythical projection'.[12]

Recognising the necessity of working from within a zone of transcendental violence, or the language of ontology, signals the first precaution for shifting focus toward the ethical relation. The second precaution involves a reflection on how the place of truth conditions the way in which the ethical relation might get opened or closed. For while the *Bringing Them Home* report clearly articulates its aims toward the call for justice, this call is hard to dissociate from the directive for truth. Of course, the testimonials are concerned with truth, but they are not of the same order as the 'regimes of truth' governing legal hearings. Some critics argue that the credibility of the stolen generations as a collective narrative is weakened by not paying heed to the report as objective truth in precisely the way that the report deemed obstructive to the task of listening and healing.[13] Nevertheless, it is worth

---

7   On the one hand, Levinas is aware of this, as he cites the problem as raised in *Totality and Infinity*, but on the other hand, he continues to insist that the ethical relation will be answerable within a discourse of phenomenology.

8   J. Derrida, 'Violence and Metaphysics: An Essay on the Thought of Emmanuel Levinas', trans. A. Bass, in *Writing and Difference* (Chicago, IL: University of Chicago Press, 1978), pp. 79–153 [Fr. 1964]. This quotation, p. 124.

9   Ibid., p. 125.

10   Ibid., p. 128.

11   Ibid.

12   D. Cornell, *The Philosophy of the Limit* (New York and London: Routledge, 1992), p. 55.

13   See B. Attwood, '"Learning About the Truth": The Stolen Generations Narrative', in B.Attwood and F. MacGowan (eds), *Telling Stories: Indigenous History and Memory in Australia and New Zealand* (Sydney: Allen and Unwin, 2001), pp. 183–212. Robert Manne makes the point that although some of the claims in the report were not as well substantiated

briefly outlining the role that 'truth' plays in public discussions about the report, as to dismiss the call for truth, might ironically dismiss the call for justice.

Public debates about the report all centre on certain truth claims, which John Morton identifies as 'three substantive matters':

> 1) statistics (how many Aboriginal people were separated from their families?); 2) definition (was the removal policy truly genocidal?); and 3) circumstances (were the children truly stolen and deprived of their heritage, or were they rescued from dire predicaments and given fresh chances in life?)[14]

These are certainly the issues raised in Australia's highly publicised 'history wars'. Questioning the veracity of the term 'stolen', tabloid newspaper columnist, Andrew Bolt repeatedly asked academic, Robert Manne – in the debate staged at Melbourne's 2006 Writers Festival – to show him 'just 10 Aboriginal children who were removed from their families because of their Aboriginality'. Bolt couched his rhetorical repetition of the question in terms that suggested removals were based on welfare considerations, while Manne provided detailed documentation to demonstrate how the removal of 'half caste' children from their families was part of a wider scheme to 'bleach out the colour' of Aboriginal Australia.[15] Manne presented his argument by including legislation, letters from police officers involved in removals, and personal testimonies amongst other evidence. Lapping up the tabloid rhythm of the debate, Bolt remained unconcerned by Manne's charge that 'he [Bolt] does not even pretend to have conducted serious research into' the issue. Even though the audience were largely sympathetic to Manne's position, journalist Martin Flanagan, states that his argument became too refined for such a forum. Public debates and newspapers do not readily accommodate the nuances, the stratified levels of interpreting archival materials and historical periods, let alone working with different orders of analysis in

---

as they could have been, this does not at all undermine injustice perpetrated on the children and their families that were subject to such State removal. R. Manne, *In Denial: The Stolen Generations and the Right* (Melbourne: Black Inc., 2001).

14 J. Morton, 'Race, Reciprocity, Reconciliation: Stolen Children and the Elementary Structures of Justice in Australia', unpublished manuscript, p. 3. Manne estimates that between 1910 and 1970 there were between 20,000–25,000 Aboriginal children separated from their families (*In Denial*, p. 27.). He also discusses the meaning of genocide and details some of the circumstances in which children were removed from their families. In 'Learning the Truth about the Stolen Generations', Attwood also discusses disputes surrounding these figures. But, disputes about numbers, in my view, detracts from the singularity of trauma experienced for each child and each member of a family affected by forced removal. There is sufficient evidence documenting the practices and policies of child removal as systematic, where even the most modest estimates on numbers are unpardonable. See footnote below.

15 The policy of biological absorption was openly and overtly practised prior to the Second World War. Manne cites documents from a conference of leading administrators in Aboriginal Affairs in 1937 in which A. O.Neville made the claim that the 'full blacks' would be extinct within one hundred years, but 'half castes' were 'quick breeders'. A. O. Neville put his case to the conference: 'Are we going to have a population of one million blacks in the Commonwealth or are we going to merge them into our white community and eventually forget that there were any Aborigines in Australia?' Cited in Manne, *In Denial*, p. 40.

the quest for the truth of a matter. As argued in Chapter Two, such differentiation is vital for sorting through the messiness of *not* situating identity as prior to the categories from which they acquire their meaning. The stolen generations are no exception here. The lived reality and experiences of the stolen generations are inextricably bound and inscribed by the conceptual and institutional frameworks that marked the children in question as other, including the abhorrent administrative measures that deployed zoological terminology to make distinctions between 'full bloods', 'half castes', 'quadroons', 'octoroons' and so on. Little wonder that skin colour became seen as a cause of shame and a reason for not identifying as Aboriginal.[16] Yet, what exceeds any attempt to contain the stolen generations' narrative to a truth war about identity and history (in terms of numbers, definitions, and circumstances) is the *interruption* of the singular voice that asks to be heard. This interruption can easily remain below the level of audibility when official narratives of history remain closed.

This chapter argues that the calls from *singular* others in the *Bringing Them Home* report *remain* and will always remain as testimony that asks for a hearing beyond 'objective truth' – responsibility. These singular calls remain whether they coalesce with official narratives or not. The task then becomes one of keeping *open* to the interruption of such calls, in order to listen, and in order to respond. A responsible response, nevertheless, requires an engagement with sorting through entangled relations between truth, law and justice. We will engage with this muddle by focusing on the singular relation between self and other. While Levinas helps us turn our gaze from a self-conscious ego to that which puts the ego in question, we recognised earlier that we must submit to the language of ontology in the process of doing so. Yet such necessity does not prevent the possibility of considering the thought that it is the ethical relation 'that sets language in motion'.[17]

Ethics as an openness to the Other

The interest in being as the site of intelligibility, Levinas argues, disallows thinkers like Heidegger and Husserl to attend to the thought that the intentional

---

16 Feelings of shame are well documented in the testimonies given in *Bringing Them Home*. This is evident in Paul's story. In many cases, the foster homes and carers were instrumental in promoting the idea that dark skin was something about which one was to be ashamed.

17 In his paper, 'At This Very Moment in This Work Here I am', trans. R. Berezdivin, in R. Bernasconi and S. Critchley (eds), *Re-Reading Levinas* (Bloomington and Indianapolis: Indiana University Press, 1991), pp. 11–48 [Fr. 1980], Derrida states that he 'admires' how Levinas states that 'Responsibility … is probably the essence of language' (p. 25, emphasis added). As Derrida goes on to say, 'Even though language can also be that which, bringing back to presence, to the same, to the economy of being, etc., has not surely got its essence in that responsibility, responsive [to and for] the other as a past which will never have been present, nevertheless it "is" such responsibility that sets language in motion. Without that [ethical] responsibility there would be no language, but it is never sure that language itself surrenders itself to the responsibility that makes it possible [surrenders to its simply probable essence]: it may always [and to a certain extent it is probably even ineluctable that it will] betray it, tending to enclose it within the same' (brackets in original).

consciousness of an ego is accompanied by an unintentional consciousness. Alongside phenomenological reflections of an intentional consciousness, there is the remainder of a non-intentional consciousness, a 'non-objectivising knowledge' that passively accompanies intentional consciousness through time without 'any wilful aim' or attributes.[18] This type of consciousness is a form of *mauvaise conscience* – an unhappy consciousness – one that is 'not yet at the stage of willing, and prior to any fault, in its non-intentional identification, identity recoils before its affirmation'.[19] As pure passivity, the unintentional consciousness 'precedes formulation of any metaphysical ideas on the subject'.[20] In this space, if we can call it a space, before concern for one's own being, one must respond to one's right to be, in which Levinas situates unintentional consciousness as opening a being's concern for an *Other*:

> My being-in-the-world or 'my place in the sun', my being at home, have these not also been the usurpation of spaces belonging to the other man whom I have already oppressed or starved, or driven out into a third world; are they not acts of repulsing, excluding, exiling, stripping, killing? Pascal's 'my place in the sun' marks the beginning of the image of the usurpation of the whole earth. *A fear for all violence and murder my existing might generate, in spite of its conscious and intentional innocence* [emphasis added]. A fear which reaches back past my 'self-consciousness' in spite of whatever moves are made toward a *bonne conscience* by pure perseverance in being. It is the fear of occupying someone else's place with the *Da* of *Dasein*; it is the inability to occupy a place, a profound utopia.[21]

Even though Levinas's ethics concerns the singular relation between self and other, there is a striking resonance between this passage, which underscores the fear of usurping the Other *beyond* intentional innocence, and current public debates regarding Australia's response as a nation to the stories of the stolen generations. In this regard, the hegemonic propagation of a *bonne conscience* governing the self-consciousness of the (White) Australian nation is constantly disrupted by its *mavaise conscience* within. Of course, one does not have to respond to the call of the other, or pay heed to this unintentional consciousness, but the *Bringing Them Home* report has prompted an unprecedented number of singular and collective responses to the testimonies recounted. Apart from ministerial responses tabled in parliament, and responses by community leaders, academics and public intellectuals in Australia's newspapers, journals and magazines, thousands of individual Australians have registered their apologies to the stolen generations in the form of 'sorry books', an

---

18 Ibid., p. 79.

19 Ibid., p. 81.

20 Ibid., p. 82.

21 Ibid., p. 87. In footnote 6, which refers to the phrase 'my being at home', Hand states that Levinas is alluding to Heidegger here. He notes Levinas's move away from Heidegger's concern with an existent coming to exist for itself. According to Levinas, while Heidegger links unintentional consciousness to the temporal and historical forgetting of Being, he primarily opens the question of a being concerned for its own being, not that of the other. However, in *Totality and Infinity* (p. 33), Lingis notes the same phrase as an allusion to Hegel, also expressing the concern for the way in which an existent concretely comes to exist for itself.

initiative prompted by the former Government's refusal to issue an apology, as a nation, to the stolen generations.[22] Each year, since 1998, 26 May is commemorated as Sorry Day. In other words, many Australians have responded to the summons to *first listen* to these singular stories, and have heeded the call to respond to this segment of the nation's heritage. At the same time, we must ask whether such a form of saying sorry has become a ritualised rule that in effect annuls the act of apology. If one says sorry out of duress, blind obedience to perceived duty, or because one might gain popularity from doing so, can we really count this as a genuine act of apology? We will return to this problem shortly.

In the last ten years, the most glaring omission within all these responses, was from Australia's former Prime Minister, John Howard and his Government – the legal successors of this nation's past policies and practices. On 13 February 2008, the newly appointed Prime Minister, Kevin Rudd, delivered the long awaited official apology.[23] It was a momentous occasion for Australia, with thousands of people gathering in public to watch Rudd deliver. As media attempted to capture the national mood and take the pulse of the response to the apology, the outpouring of emotion was palpable. But it would be wrong to presume that the spectres of White Australia's Black history could be readily buried by this act on February 13th. For the very day before the national apology, those who had gathered together outside Canberra to witness Rudd's speech had organised a protest against the Government's intervention in Aboriginal communities in the Northern Territory and this had barely stirred a whisper in the media.[24] If this did not remind us that the spectre of a mean spirited Australia could arise at any time, there were other speeches in parliament waiting to do so. The tears and cheers following Rudd's speech barely subsided, when the leader of the opposition, Brendan Nelson, echoed the sentiments of the former Prime Minister.[25]

Responding to a heritage in the disadjusted time of the present

Nelson's speech, like John Howard's infamous speech at the Australian Reconciliation Convention in 1997, typifies the conservative position in Australia's history wars. Howard had claimed that he 'did not believe that current generations of Australians could be held accountable for or regarded as guilty for the acts of earlier generations over which they had no control'.[26] Whilst Nelson offered an apology, it

---

22 See H. Gooder and J. M. Jacobs, 'Belonging and non-Belonging: the Apology in a Reconciling Nation', in A. Blunt and C. McEwan (eds), *Postcolonial Geographies* (New York: Continuum, 2002), pp. 200–13.

23 The full speech of the national apology delivered in the Australian parliament and televised throughout the nation, can be accessed at http://www.pm.gov.au/media/Speech/2008/speech_0073.cfm.

24 See footnote 5, Chapter One.

25 Brendan Nelson's response to the apology can be accessed at http://www.theage.com.au/news/national/bfull-textb-brendan-nelsons-speech/2008/02/13/1202760363287.html.

26 J. Howard, Opening Address to the Australian Reconciliation Convention, Melbourne, May, 1997 cited in Frow, 'A Politics of Stolen Time'.

was immediately undermined by his claim that 'Our generation does not own these actions, nor should it feel guilt for what was done in many, but not all cases, with the best of intentions.'[27] The presupposition that the past occupies a discrete temporality from the present and future is fundamental to the conservative response to the stolen generations in particular and to the conservative attitude concerning the status of the place of Aboriginal people in Australia's heritage more generally. Such response also holds that one cannot judge one epoch from the point of view of another, presuming that such a totalising and discrete form of periodisation is possible – a presumption that the preceding chapter renders highly problematic. Opponents to such conservatism stress connections between the past and present, explaining the current levels of poor health, well being and social inclusion of Aboriginal people as emerging from past injustices. Moreover, the call for apology and acknowledgement of Australia's past stresses the direct benefits that present generations enjoy from past violence. Tessa Morris-Suzuki's concept of 'implication' aptly summarises such an attitude toward the past:

> Implication means the existence of a conscious connection to the past, but also the reality of being (in a legal sense) 'an accessory after the fact'. It is the status of those who have not stolen land from others, but who live on stolen land; the status of those who have not participated in massacres, but have participated in the process by which the memory of those massacres has been obliterated; the status of those who have not injured others, but allow the consequences of past injury to go unaddressed. Implication means that the prejudices, which sustained past acts of aggression live on into the present, and will lodge themselves in the minds of the present generation unless we make the effort to remove them. We who live in the present did not create the violence and hatred of the past. But the violence and hatred of the past, to some degree, created us. It formed the material world and the ideas with which we live, and will continue to do so unless we take active steps to unmake their consequences.[28]

This notion of implication suggests that everybody's relation to the present calls for a reckoning with the circumstances they have inherited. This way of situating the past to the present and future goes a long way toward responding to the heritage of colonial Australia. It is an essential step in coming to terms with justice for others. Yet, this logic of the past in the present still relies on a certain metaphysics of (full) presence, which can easily nullify the necessity of working through the 'always already' literal *dislocation* of time that keeps open the space for *fresh judgment* and *decision* when responding to a heritage. Recalling the previous chapter's discussion of hauntology as situating the here and now as dis-adjusted to itself, we will move toward a space where we can consider the dis-located time in more detail. In this chapter this disadjusted time of the present will be related to the space of justice, where the other calls me into question.

---

27 Nelson, http://www.theage.com.au/news/national/bfull-textb-brendan-nelsons-speec h/2008/02/13/1202760363287.html.

28 T. Morris-Suzuki quoted in M. Hokari, 'Globalising Aboriginal Reconciliation: Indigenous Australians and Asian (Japanese) Migrants', *Cultural Studies Review*, 9 (2003): 84–101. This quotation, p. 98.

Let's think back to the figures of the ghost and the spectre from the previous chapter. Neither living nor dead, the ghost troubles the security of the borders of the present. And without a material body for itself, the spectre struggles for possession of the body's spirit. Australia is haunted by the ghosts of its past, who refuse to stay buried in the foundational spectres of its virtual body. When Peggy Kamuf translates *hantise* to haunting for Derrida's *Specters of Marx*, she notes that the French word also 'has the common sense of an obsession, a constant fear, a fixed idea, or a nagging memory'.[29] Such obsession and fear reveal themselves in the history wars in Australia where several spectres compete over a politics of memory, over heritage and the spirit of Australia's future, and indeed, whether such a struggle ought to remain within the confines of the nation state. So reckoning with the circumstances we have inherited – or the circumstances of implication as Morris-Suzuki puts it – involves reckoning with competing ghosts and spectres. We are all heirs to what has gone before us, as we are all forebears for what we pass on. But the heritage for which we take responsibility *in the name of justice* is not transparently given to us, and the twist for Derrida is that justice cannot be satisfied with bringing the past and present into '*accord*' – as if that were possible. It is easy to lose the thread of Derrida's argument here, as it is hard to dislodge common sense notions of justice as tied to notions of accord and reconciliation. It helps to recall Derrida's words from the previous chapter that an inheritance is 'never one with itself', where 'one must 'filter, sift, [and] criticize' several possibles for the same injunction.[30] That is, inheritance requires work and not the mechanical reproduction of a supposedly transparent imperative. To think about the inclination to link justice with accord it is worth briefly outlining Derrida's reading of Heidegger on this point. Then we will return to the place of apology and reconciliation in Australia's heritage.

Thought about injunction – in this case the injunction to apologise, which in turn is related to the pledge for reconciliation – is traditionally related to a notion of jointure, of bringing into accord that which is 'out of joint'. On this point, Derrida turns our attention to Heidegger, whose reflections on the present as that 'between what goes and what comes, in the middle of what leaves and what arrives, at the articulation of what absents and presents itself' situates the dislocated time of the present as that which is always ordered in the 'two directions of absence'.[31] What 'gives' jointure then, is made possible by *dis*jointure. For Heidegger, Derrida claims, the giving that consists in 'leaving to the other what properly belongs to him or her' is located in the *jointure* of the two movements of what absents itself and what presents itself. Derrida's trepidation with the emphasis on jointure lies in the tempting possibility to move from thinking the disjointed-to-the-disadjusted-to-the-unjust. For Derrida contends that *if* one translates the word *Dikë* from Heidegger's, 'The Anaximander Fragment' as '"justice," and if, as Heidegger does, *Dikë* is thought on

---

29 P. Kamuf, translator's note, *Specters of Marx*, fn2, p. 177. For an account of how the place of Aboriginality haunts modern Australia see K. Gelder and J. M. Jacobs, *Uncanny Australia: Sacredness and Identity in a Postcolonial Nation* (Melbourne: Melbourne University Press, 1998). My thanks to Glenn D'Cruz for this reference.

30 Derrida, *Specters of Marx*, p. 16.

31 Ibid., p. 25.

the basis of Being as presence, then it would turn out that "justice" is first of all, and finally, and especially *properly*, the jointure of the accord'.[32] On this account, the space that adjoins the two movements (between presence and absence) could imply that injustice is to be located in disjointure.[33] But the paradox, as Derrida sees it, is that disjointure is *necessary* for staying open to the calls from incoming others. To distinguish between the two opposing possibilities of this disjointure, or disjunction – between 'injustice' and the opening to the other – a deconstructive move becomes necessary. It is necessary so that the move to adjoin the space of the disadjusted (Heidegger's 'favor ... of the accord that gathers or collects while harmonizing'[34]) does not *close* the disjointure, because such a disjointure is the necessary condition of possibility for justice ('the relation to others').

To return to the injunction for reconciliation and the apology in Australia, we can certainly see the injustice lodged within the disjunction between the nation's past and future. Indeed, like Hamlet, succeeding governments might curse the day they were called to set things right. And setting things right within the terms of political interventions currently debated in Australia, unsurprisingly, situates justice with accord. No doubt, this is why articulating ethics and justice in terms of disjointure would trouble many critics concerned with social transformation, as it seems to go against the very promise for emancipation. This is to say, to think justice through disjointure is counterintuitive, so it is worth pondering this point.

As argued in the previous chapter, to believe we can know in advance what an emancipated society looks like is not only impossible, but dangerous. To say what communism *is* or what democracy *is*, presumes a presence for that which can only remain spectral. The same goes for reconciliation. It can to some extent function as a regulating ideal, but to presume we know its empirical actuality would be to pre-set a calculable programme that too readily relinquishes negotiation with a meaning that remains internally divided and multiple. To presume to know in advance what political programme will achieve reconciliation relinquishes negotiation with keeping a space open for that which must remain incalculable and beyond anticipation. It is not as if reconciliation is achieved now that the new Federal Government has apologised, *as crucial as an apology is* to reckoning with injustices of the past. For without asking after the heritage of the concept of reconciliation, or without interrogating the spectral struggles for possession of reconciliation's meaning, there is always the danger of reducing politics to a pre-programmed set of actions that can be ticked off like any other 'to do' list. If politics and ethics remain as nothing more than ticking off a pre-set list of actions, justice becomes confused with resting 'on the good conscience of having done one's duty, [and so] it loses its future'.[35] This is

---

32 Ibid., p. 27. In 'The Anaximander Fragment', where Heidegger allegedly gives a more literal German translation of the Greek fragment, the English translation reads: 'But that from which things arise also gives rise to their passing away, according to what is necessary; for things render justice and pay penalty to one another for their injustice, according to the ordinance of time' (p. 20).

33 Derrida, *Specters of Marx*, p. 27.

34 Ibid.

35 Ibid., p. 28.

precisely how the Howard government had appropriated the term in its articulation of 'practical reconciliation'. Like any other signifier, reconciliation can be appropriated for purposes contrary to the spirit of its promise.

Reconciliation, calculability and the law

As Andrew Schaap[36] notes, suspicions of reconciliation as a unifying banner for the Australian nation point out that the term assumes some kind of prior social cohesion. As he states, the 'term is meant to encapsulate the idea that reconciliation necessarily invokes both an original unity that has never actually existed and an ultimate unity that remains to come in order to make politics possible in the present'.[37] Following Michael Phillips, Schaap refers to the ever-problematic '"embarrassment of the first person plural"' whenever reconciliation is invoked. This inevitably raises the issue over the legal legitimacy of colonisation, whereby the initial 'we' forming the Australian nation is called into question. Negotiating the reconstitution of a 'we' that recognises the original inhabitants of the land has thus become of utmost importance for bodies such as the Council for Aboriginal Reconciliation (CAR).

In 2000, CAR produced the *Australian Declaration Towards Reconciliation* (hereafter, the *Declaration*), where the opening lines read: 'We, the peoples of Australia, of many origins as we are, make a commitment to go on together in a spirit of reconciliation.'[38] After acknowledging the Aboriginal and Torres Strait Islander peoples as original custodians of the land, that the land was colonised without treaty or consent, and that there is a continuing 'spiritual relationship between the land and its first people', the *Declaration* shifts focus to reconciliation for past injustices. The Declaration then states that while 'steps have been taken' to deal with Australia's past, 'many steps remain as we learn our shared histories'. At this point it is worth reflecting upon how the question of shared histories feeds back into preceding statements that concern questions of legitimacy and law between the custodians of the land and the colonisers.

Recognising colonisation without treaty or consent brings to the surface the violent past of Australia's history that had remained suppressed in the national imaginary up until relatively recently.[39] As Paul Patton notes, with no pact between colonisers and the Indigenous people of this land, Australia is different from other 'settler' countries such as Canada or New Zealand.[40] The absence of a treaty gained significant publicity in 1992, when the high court passed the *Mabo* decision on a

---

36 A. Schapp, 'The Proto-politics of Reconciliation: Lefort and the Aporia of Forgiveness in Arendt and Derrida', *Australian Journal of Political Science*, 41, (Dec. 2006): 615–30.

37 Ibid, p. 616.

38 Council for Aboriginal Reconciliation, *Australian Declaration Towards Reconciliation*, 2000, http://www.austlii.edu.au/au/other/IndigLRes/car/2000/12/pg3.htm.

39 The most commonly cited and widely recognised text for opening to a broader public the contest to Australia's foundational narrative is W. E. H. Stanner's, *The 1968 Boyer Lectures: After the Dreaming* (Sydney: The Australian Broadcasting Commission, 1969).

40 P. Patton, 'Mabo and Australian Society: Towards a Postmodern Republic', *The Australian Journal of Anthropology*, 6, 12 (Aug 1995), p. 83.

land rights claim, declaring that the settlers illegitimately and inappropriately proclaimed Australia as *terra nullius* – literally translating to 'no man's land'. Such a conception, with recourse to common law at the time of colonisation, was made on the assumption that the Aboriginal people were insufficiently civilised to have a notion of property, and were presumed to live without law.[41] As Patton claims, the Mabo case tests legal and political recognition of cultural difference insofar as the principle upon which British sovereignty was founded became recognised as wrong. Yet, while the decision recognised that Aboriginal and Islander law existed prior to British colonisation – opening the door for recognising native title in land rights claims – the common law's authority remains sovereign over Indigenous forms of law. This is to say, the Crown can still extinguish native title.[42] So on the one hand, the Mabo decision illustrates how recognition of a past wrong in the foundation of the nation state still can be rearticulated to reaffirm the legitimacy of (common) law. But on the other hand, the return to the foundation begs the question of the legitimacy and authority of 'common' law itself.

Law as founding violence and the undeconstructability of justice

To pursue this line of thought further, we can demonstrate that the founding violence of Australia as a nation state is seeped in the bloodshed of frontier violence, and wrongful dispossession and degradation of Aboriginal peoples.[43] Yet the recognition that something is rotten in the state of Australia – as significant as such recognition is – eclipses the question that something might be rotten in the very form of the state. Walter Benjamin tackles this question in his famous essay, 'Critique of Violence'. Derrida takes up Benjamin's questions as part of his keynote colloquium address for 'Deconstruction and the Possibility of Justice', delivered in 1989 at the Cardozo Law School.[44] Derrida argues that what often confuses law with justice is that the former is an authorised force. By interrogating this authority, Derrida will help keep the question of justice in focus when considering current debates about reconciliation and forgiveness. In maintaining the need to distinguish law from justice, Derrida

---

41 Unsurprisingly historical archives show that the declaration of *terra nullius* was not as homogeneous and consistent from state to state, or indeed between different governors and officials. In his meticulous research on the issue, research that was instrumental in providing evidence for the *Mabo* decision, Henry Reynolds uncovered much dissension about the status of Aboriginal peoples' relation to land and property, which suggests there was an awareness of that *terra nullius* was an inappropriate way of describing the Australian continent. See H. Reynolds, *Aboriginal Sovereignty: Reflections on Race, State and Nation* (Sydney: Allen and Unwin, 1996) and *Why Weren't We Told? A Personal Search for the Truth About our History* (Melbourne: Viking, 1999).

42 For an account of how the *Native Title Act* after the Mabo decision is viewed as a legislative failure and undermines land rights, see G. Foley, 'The Australian Labor Party and the *Native Title Act*', in Aileen Moreton Robinson (ed.), *Sovereign Subjects: Indigenous Sovereignty Matters* (Crows Nest: Allen & Unwin, 2007), pp. 118–39.

43 See H. Reynolds, *The Other side of the Frontier: Aboriginal Resistance to the European Invasion of Australia* (Sydney: University of New South Wales Press, 2007) [1981].

44 Derrida, 'Force of Law'.

asks what the difference might be between a legitimate or just 'force of law' and the 'violence that one always deems unjust'. He probes further:

> How are we to distinguish between the force of law of a legitimate power and the supposedly originary violence that must have established this authority and that could not itself be authorized by any anterior legitimacy, so that, in this initial moment, it is neither legal nor illegal – or, others would quickly say, neither just nor unjust?[45]

In other words, the founding moment of law, 'even when there haven't been those spectacular genocides, expulsion or deportations that so often accompany the foundation of states' is for that instituting moment, non-law.[46] In drawing our attention to this, Derrida points to the fact that law is deconstructible, which, as ought to be clear by now, is not bad news for politics. Far from aiming to destroy principles of law, deconstruction aims at calling law to responsibility for how law is founded and for the way in which justice exceeds and is excluded by it. It is precisely because laws are 'constructed on interpretable or transformable textual strata (and that is the history of law [*droit*], its possible and necessary transformation, sometimes its amelioration), or because its ultimate foundation is by definition unfounded' that it is deconstructible. On the other hand, Derrida situates justice as *undeconstructible*, a statement that, as Derrida is well aware, appears scandalous. As John Caputo asks,

> Undeconstructible Justice? … What is that if not a transcendental signifier that detaches itself from the chain of signifiers, that claims for itself a special exemption from the quasi law of *différance*, as if the worst injustice, the most bloody and unjustifiable transgressions of justice, are not committed daily in the name of justice, under the protection of the name 'justice'; as if 'justice' alone succeeded in maintaining its identity and never became injustice; as if the name 'justice' were one name and meant some single thing.[47]

Caputo has a point. But he also trusts that Derrida might be on to something in reserving a special place for justice. Justice does not stand alone as a concept in Derrida's 'Force of Law'. In distinguishing justice from law, Derrida draws our attention to the *interval* between the two. To situate justice as undeconstructible, it would somehow have to *exceed* what we have so far identified as the doubled and divided nature of meaning. From what has been argued in previous chapters, this would seem impossible. Yet it is this 'experience of the impossible' – that Derrida signals elsewhere as the least bad way of defining deconstruction – where deconstruction begins its work. Law's desire for the universal and for calculating what is to be done must operate with recourse to general principles. In contrast, justice, like Levinas's ethical relation, reserves openness to the singular – to the other who slips beneath the calculability of law and cannot be subsumed by a general principle. An identity politics that conflated law with justice, would lose sight of why law will always be inadequate to justice, because justice comes to law in the singular. As Caputo puts it:

45　Ibid., p. 6.
46　Ibid., p. 35.
47　Caputo, *Against Ethics*, p. 86.

> Laws are always oversized or undersized, too sweeping or too narrow, more or less bad fits. A perfect set of laws would have to be cut to fit; it would have to mention everybody by name. ... A perfect set of laws would be like a map so perfect that it would match in size the region of which it is the map. That would be very inconvenient and spell the end of law. It would fulfil the purpose (*finis*) of law, like a kind of *pleroma*, but it would also finish it off (*terminatio*) since generalizing goes to the heart of what law is. A Book of Justice, a book in which the distance between justice and law would be closed, would be quite a size.[48]

Exposing the gap between law and justice is not part of a strategy to undermine struggles for legislative change, or to neglect legal recognition for past wrongs. For example, the *Bringing Them Home* report's recommendation to set up national compensation schemes for those children forcibly removed from their parents *is vital* for dealing with the damages incurred by State practices and policies. To date, there has been only one successful case in suing the Government by a person of the stolen generation.[49] A national compensation fund would certainly perform a crucial role in acknowledging the past wrongs of child removal as systematic. It would help to reduce the emotional trauma of stolen generation members having to present themselves in a court of law on a case-by-case basis. And it would reduce the lengthy deliberations and monetary court costs that individual cases must currently bear. A national compensatory fund would recognise the violation of human rights evident in the stories of the stolen generations. Law in this instance provides the element of calculation to deal with the unjust practices of child removal. As Derrida says, 'it is just there be law'. But, he adds,

> Law (droit) is not justice. ... [J]ustice is incalculable, it requires us to calculate with the incalculable; and aporetic experiences are the experiences, as improbable as they are necessary, of justice, that is to say of moments in which the decision between just and unjust is never insured by a rule.[50]

So while it is just in the legal sense that there be a compensatory fund for the stolen generations, it would not be just in the ethical sense to state that justice *is done* on receipt of acknowledgement, apology or reparation. Justice's work is never done. As with the recognition that law is deconstructible, the impossibility of justice's arrival is also not bad news for politics. With this in mind, let us return to the issue of reconciliation and apology.

---

48 Ibid., p. 88.

49 On 1 August 2007, Bruce Trevorrow was awarded compensation by the Supreme Court of South Australia. Before this case, there were five unsuccessful cases. These cases are summarised in C. Cunneen and J. Grix, *The Limitations of Litigation in Stolen Generations Cases* (Canberra: Australian Institute of Aboriginal and Torres Strait Islander Studies, 2004).

50 Derrida, 'Force of Law', p. 16.

Reconciliation: from the calculability of law to the incalculability and justice

The recognition of the founding violence that preserves the legitimacy of law after the event of its institution alerts us to the fact that we need to take responsibility for its interpretation, its reinterpretation and transformation. The aforementioned cases of Mabo and the stolen generations both reinterpret past laws and practices in view of making the current law more just. Most proponents of identity politics would have no trouble in agreeing with the imperative to calculate with law on these issues. The trouble begins with the imperative to *not* measure justice solely by law, and to situate justice within the order of the incalculable. The interval between law and justice must be maintained; as it is this interval that keeps watch over the confused conservative belief that what can be deemed just is reducible to what the law is. Because the distinction between law and justice is not pure, because each pole of the distinction is regulated and kept in check by the other, the aporetic relation between law and justice 'infinitely distributes itself', giving us pause to negotiate with the incalculability of justice.[51] Derrida identifies three examples where aporias of this relation arise. Let us focus on the first.

The first aporia, named the 'épokhè of the rule' arises in the demand for 'fresh judgment' through unique interpretation of pre-existing law. While judgments have to be made according to the law, Derrida argues that the role of the judge – in order to make a *just* decision – cannot be a mere instrument that calculates. That would be equivalent to punching evidence into a computer to determine a verdict: this would be akin to the bureaucrat on *Little Britain* who repeatedly states, 'computer says, no'. Each decision 'requires an absolutely unique interpretation, which no existing, coded rule can or ought to guarantee absolutely'. Hence, for a decision to be just, the pre-existing law, which must ultimately be followed, must also be momentarily suspended so that a 'fresh judgment' can be made in 'a reinstituting act of interpretation.' This does not mean that a judge makes a decision without reference to any law or convention. The decision is made *between* existing law *and* the call for fresh judgment. In both the Mabo case and cases involving the stolen generations, judges have been bound to make their decisions by pre-existing law, yet the calls for justice, to which such judgments remain bound have certainly brought the tension of this aporia to the surface. In the Mabo case, the reinstituting act of interpretation involved a new judgment on the wrongful interpretation of *terra nullius* within the parameters of existing common law. Interestingly, the evidence presented in the Mabo judgment was documentation from which the judges could readily calculate.[52] The requirements for objective evidence spoke within the 'regimes of truth' comprehensible in a court of law. Significantly, however, this ruling by no means indicates that justice has arrived for Indigenous people, as will be indicated below. Still the Mabo re-interpretation of *terra nullius* opened new dimensions within the calculability of law.

---

51 Ibid., p. 22.

52 B. Attwood, 'Unsettling Pasts: Reconciliation and History in Settler Australia', *Postcolonial Studies*, 8, 3 (2005): 243–59. My thanks to Claudia Haake for this reference.

The aporia between law and justice in cases involving the stolen generations, however, have posed a greater burden on the reinstituting act of fresh judgments within the confines of calculative, pre-existing law. This is largely due to the subjective delivery of evidence and the interpretation of intentionality with 'prevailing standards of the times'. Yet the successful Trevorrow case called for a fresh judgment on how 'prevailing standards of the times' were to be *re*interpreted. In previous cases, judges argued that the missionaries and officials involved in child removal acted out of supposedly benevolent welfare considerations in line with 'prevailing standards of the times'. As racist as this sounds in current times, governments and other authorities believed, so the argument goes, that it would be in the best interests of 'mixed race' children to grow up with white families. The Trevorrow case focused on evidence suggesting that in the 1950s 'it was generally understood among psychiatrists and psychologists that removing children from their primary carer was likely to cause harm to the child'.[53] This fresh judgment was able to oppose prevailing interpretations of law that could not adequately deal with the unjust treatment of child separation from their mothers in particular, and families more generally. It remains to be seen if this new judgment will lead to the setting up of compensation schemes, as some states within Australia have already done.

Yet, as earlier mentioned, even if a compensation fund were set up in the light of this reinstituted act of interpretation, it would be excessively hasty to presume that justice would be done. Acknowledgement of past injustice is crucial to the process of healing, but to locate justice in the present – to announce, for example, that reconciliation is here – would nullify the necessity for justice to remain as that which is always 'to come'. This brings us to the second aporia relating to the interval between the calculability of law and the incalculability of justice.

Apology and the impossible possibility of forgiveness

In the event of the government acknowledging responsibility for such past injustices and apologising to the Indigenous peoples of Australia, the interval between the poles of calculability and incalculability are not to be closed. Rather the interval obliges a reckoning once again with the aporetic nature of the relation between law and justice as a means for keeping justice open. As indicated already it would be presumptuous and naïve to believe in a linear progression that moves from apology and reparation to forgiveness and reconciliation. So let us consider what might be involved in the decision to forgive, as this is what sits between the act of apology and the move toward reconciliation. Situating the decision to forgive in terms of the second aporia of justice identified in 'Force of Law' can also help clarify the misunderstanding that the undecidability involved in making a decision suggests that decisions are thus made without deliberation.

---

53 J. Burnside, 'Stolen Generation: Time for Change', http://www.australiansall.com.au/stolen-generation-time-for-a-change/, accessed 11/10/2007.

When Derrida contends that lodged within every decision is the 'ghost of the undecidable' it is not to suggest that the undecidable is 'merely the oscillation or tension between two decisions' – to forgive or not to forgive, for example.

> It is the experience of that which, though heterogeneous, foreign to the order of the calculable and the rule, is still obliged – it is of obligation that we must speak – to give itself up to the impossible decision, while taking account of law and rules.[54]

The impossible decision we are concerned with here is the decision to forgive what is unforgivable. Derrida's work on the aporia of forgiveness has produced much perplexity around the paradox summed up in the sentence, 'forgiveness forgives only the unforgivable'.[55] Set in the context of the international 'geopolitical scene' where acts of repentance, confession, forgiveness and apology has 'accelerated' in recent years, within which we can include the setting of the scene for the apology to the Indigenous peoples of Australia, Derrida draws our attention to the double and contradictory injunction at the heart of the concept's heritage. For taking responsibility for a heritage is not only a reckoning with the spectres that compete for meaning over what has happened – on the land in which we live, for instance – but is also a reckoning with the concepts that guide how we come to terms with historical events. The language of forgiveness, Derrida notes, emerges from powerful European or 'biblical' traditions – '"Abrahamic" culture and that of a philosophical humanism, and more precisely a cosmopolitanism born from a graft of stoicism with Pauline Christianity'.[56] The double injunction stemming from this inherited concept contrasts *unconditional forgiveness*, on the one hand, with *conditional forgiveness* on the other.

For Derrida any serious reckoning with apology and reconciliation must deal with both sides of the injunction. Beginning with the conditional logic, the logic upon which current scenes of reconciliation stage themselves, forgiveness is considered *on the condition* that an apology is first delivered. It is only *upon* apology, upon repentance of the fault committed, guilt acknowledged and reparations calculated in proportion to the severity of the crime, that reconciliation could *then* begin. In the public sphere, such language about apology and forgiveness regulates much talk about national reconciliation. As the *Australian Declaration Towards Reconciliation* states:

> As we walk the journey of healing, one part of the nation apologises and expresses its sorrow and sincere regret for the injustices of the past, so that the other part accepts the apologies and forgives.

As Richard Bernstein notes, without dismissing the importance and necessity of public apology, Derrida questions the appropriateness of speaking about forgiveness in the context of national reconciliation. Furthermore, the 'syntactical ambiguity'

---

54 Derrida, 'Force of Law', p. 24.

55 J. Derrida, *On Cosmopolitanism and Forgiveness* (New York: Routledge, 2001), p. 32.

56 Ibid., p. 31.

between whether one is forgiving *something* – 'a crime, a fault, a wrong' – or *someone* complicates the request for forgiveness. If it is *someone*, does one ask forgiveness of the 'victim, or some absolute witness, of God'? Derrida notes in passing that the church of France asked for forgiveness of God rather than before people, or the victims of the Jewish community, for example. While suspending this complicated ambiguity between 'the question of "what?" and the question of "whom?"', Derrida poses the following hypothesis. If forgiveness is given on the condition of repentance, and the culpable person 'mends his ways', is it still appropriate to speak of forgiveness, in the light of the fact that the guilty one is now someone other through the act of repentance and acceptance of a new obligation? He asks:

> In order for there to be forgiveness, must one not on the contrary forgive both the fault and the guilty as such, where the one and the other remain as irreversible as the evil, as evil itself, and being capable of repeating itself, unforgivably, without transformation, without amelioration, without repentance or promise? Must one not maintain that an act of forgiveness worthy of its name, if there ever is such a thing, must forgive the unforgivable, and without condition? And that such unconditionality is also inscribed, like its contrary, namely the condition of repentance, in 'our' heritage?[57]

Of course, this is a very difficult proposition to hear. As with Derrida's positioning of justice with disjointure, the thought of an unconditional forgiveness is counterintuitive. Yet Derrida insists that any forgiveness worthy of the name must reckon with this unconditionality at the heart of the concept's heritage. To do so, Derrida turns to the unforgivable cases where it seems irrefutable that one should not forgive. Considering Vladmir Jankélévich's statement that 'forgiveness died in the death camps', Derrida agrees that the monstrous crimes of the death camps are indeed unforgivable and that there is no measure of punishment that could be proportional to the crimes committed.[58] Yet, Derrida maintains that it is precisely where the unforgivable is lodged that the impossibility of forgiving finds its possibility to forgive. He asks, what would we be forgiving, if we deemed an act forgivable? For Derrida forgiveness is not about the national health of a nation, a calculative means to achieve unity and reconciliation. Once again, such an impossible thought prompts further consideration.

To think through the impossibility of forgiveness as the condition of its possibility, Derrida considers once again the irreducibility and indissociability between two poles of an oppositional pair: conditional forgiveness and unconditional forgiveness. These two poles are also analogous to the pairs of calculability and incalculability, and law and justice. Conditional forgiveness belongs to an economy of exchange. If forgiveness mechanically comes with apology and automatically produces reconciliation, as if all decisions concerning forgiveness were reducible to such an element of calculation, then the *decision* to forgive is no decision at all. Exceeding the economy of exchange, as beyond calculation, unconditional forgiveness carries the weight of an impossible decision. It does not belong to the order of rationality, and it does not have an end in sight (such as reconciliation) as the condition upon which

---

57 Derrida, 'Forgiveness', *On Cosmopolitanism and Forgiveness*, p. 39.
58 Ibid., p. 37.

forgiveness will be granted. As earlier indicated, with regard to the second aporia of justice, the responsible decision must confront the abyss that remains between the orders of calculability and incalculability. As Richard Bernstein puts it:

> There is no real forgiveness unless we pass through this abyss – the experience of *trembling* when we struggle with the aporias that we confront – when we face up to the realization that forgiveness is impossible, that forgiveness forgives only the unforgivable. When Derrida tells us that forgiveness is an impossible possible, he is not playing frivolous games with us. He seeks to *intensify* the experience of decision and responsibility involved in forgiveness.[59]

Reckoning with the intensity of the decision regarding forgiveness aims to avoid a facile response to the scene of apology and reconciliation. It is not a trivial decision and for those victims and survivors – of the stolen generations in this case – the act of forgiveness in the name of national unity undermines the singularity of the experience in which the unforgivable has taken place.

On the issue of situating and naming the unforgivable, Bernstein questions Derrida's treatment of judgement. Bernstein extracts a segment from Derrida's paper on forgiveness that declares, 'forgiveness has precisely nothing to do with judgment'. Bernstein argues that there must be judgement regarding where and how one draws the line between the forgivable and unforgivable. To put this charge in the context of the present chapter, Bernstein might argue that I am making a judgement that regards child separation and removal as unforgivable. While there is judgement involved in this, I do not think that it is this type of judgement that Derrida is referring to when he declares that there is no judgement in forgiveness. Rather the act of judgement once again benefits from thinking the tension between the orders of calculability and incalculability, between law and justice. The declaration is made in the context of considering the inappropriateness of forgiveness in public discourse about national unity and reconciliation, where Derrida takes us back to consideration of the singular relation; what in this chapter is referred to as the ethical relation. Derrida asks whether it is appropriate for a third party – in the form of a mediating tertiary institution such as the State or special commission – to presume forgiveness on behalf of a victim. Courts of law might judge whether members of the stolen generations ought to receive compensation, or whether a person or body is liable for a breach of duty of care. But can the courts presume forgiveness will automatically flow from this? The preceding sentences before Derrida's declaration concerning judgement read:

> ... the anonymous body of the State or of a public institution cannot forgive. It has neither the right nor the power to do so; and besides, that would have no meaning. The representative of the State can judge, but forgiveness has precisely nothing to do with judgment.[60]

---

59 R. Bernstein, 'Derrida: The Aporia of Forgiveness?', *Constellations*, 13, 3 (2006): 394–406. This quotation, p. 398.

60 Derrida, 'On Forgiveness', *On Cosmopolitanism and Forgiveness*, p. 43.

There is a distinction here between *judgment* in the juridical process that is concerned with the calculability of law and the *decision* to forgive, which is inaccessible to law. There are singular submissions to the *Bringing Them Home* report that speak of forgiveness as part of the healing process, but there are also voices that express the inability to forgive. The secret of the dividing line between the decision to forgive or not to forgive remains. And it ought to remain. The instant of such a decision is not dependent on cognitive deliberation that surfaces with time and knowledge. Not dissimilar to the third aporia of justice identified in 'Force of Law', the decision is out of time, the 'instant of the decision is madness', and is marked with an 'urgency that obstructs the horizon of knowledge'.[61]

Paul, whose story opened the present chapter, does not say whether he forgives or does not forgive the authorities and people involved in his separation from his mother. His mother is dead, with no singular person able to forgive on her behalf. It would not be just to require forgiveness from Paul or his mother for the sake of 'national unity' or reconciliation. Yet, it is still necessary to engage with what needs to be done 'publicly, politically, juridically' for the healing process to begin. While Paul's story is inextricably related to questions of identity, the particular discontinuities and connections between truth, law and justice, and ontology, politics and ethics involve impossible decisions rather than a set of problems to be overcome for the elaboration of identity politics. To engage with these impossible decisions in terms of the aporias raised in the present chapter is not to abandon the questions of what is to be done. Rather it is to reckon with the weight and height of responsibility that accompanies the making of every ethico-political decision. Without this reckoning, we are in jeopardy of reducing the process of reconciliation to a hollow calculable programme and relinquishing the seriousness of apology. Most importantly, however, we are in danger of trivialising the unimaginable position of the victims and survivors facing the impossible task of forgiving the unforgivable.

---

61 Derrida, 'Force of Law', p. 26.

Chapter Five

Welcome Stranger:
Democracy 'to come', Autoimmunity
and Hospitality

The French phrase, *vers l'étranger* can translate into English as 'toward the stranger or foreigner, as well as to the word abroad.[1] Both Levinas and Derrida exploit this double meaning of *l'étranger* to ethical effect. As going abroad, one meaning in the Levinasian sense concerns metaphysical desire as 'going forth from a world that is familiar to us … toward an alien outside-of-oneself'.[2] The other concerns the ethical relation – the self's responsibility for the non-subsumable face of the other. As Peperzak puts it, *l'étranger* 'expresses simultaneously the foreign country from which truth comes to me and the stranger who knocks on my door in order to receive the hospitality of my home'.[3] In *Of Hospitality*, the title of Derrida's first seminar, *Question d'etranger: venue de l'etranger*, is translated to 'Coming from Abroad/ From the Foreigner'.[4] This chapter dispatches discourses of identity politics to move toward the stranger/foreigner by reserving a space for what might come from abroad in the articulation of the emancipatory promise. It will do so by engaging with what Derrida calls a 'democracy to come', while also arguing for the refugee as an exemplary figure of *l'étranger*. And it does so in order to dislodge the perfunctory manner in which identity politics privilege the *calculability* of its protocols of articulation and elaboration of the emancipatory ideal without adequately engaging with the *incalculable* dimension of decision making in the face of its own aporias.

The confrontation between the orders of calculability and incalculability emerged in the previous chapter in aporetic relations between law and justice as well as the aporetic double injunction between conditional and unconditional forgiveness. The present chapter encounters aporias between the calculability of identity politics and the incalculable promise of a 'democracy to come', by turning to Derrida's deployment of the term, autoimmunity. Borrowed from biological discourses, autoimmunity describes the process in which an organism turns against its own immune system as a means of self-protection. Alongside other Derridean

---

1   A. Peperzak, *To the Other: An Introduction to the Philosophy of Emmanuel Levinas* (Indiana: Purdue University Press, 1993), p. 39.

2   Levinas, *Totality and Infinity*, p. 33.

3   Peperzak, *To the Other*, p. 39.

4   J. Derrida and A. Dufourmantelle, *Of Hospitality: Anne Dufourmantelle invites Jacques Derrida to Respond*, trans R. Bowlby (Stanford, CA: Stanford University Press, 2000).

'infrastructures', autoimmunity offers a way of exposing the impossibility of any self-identity being proper to itself and as such the preservation of any presumed identity is always threatened by its own internal division. This threat, however, can also act as a chance for remaining open to something other than itself. In situating identity politics in terms of a 'democracy to come' and a movement toward the stranger (*vers l'etranger*), contemporary configurations of the refugee – the subject without identity papers – provides the most apt figure for thinking through such an opening. Such a figure comes without announcement or identity. Following Derrida, engaging with the figure of the refugee against the emancipatory promise calls for a detour through another aporetic double injunction – the aporia between conditional and unconditional hospitality.

Calculating identity politics with the emancipatory promise of democracy

'Democracy counts', says Derrida. '[I]t counts votes and subjects, but it does not count, it should not count, ordinary singularities: there is no *numerus clausus* for *arrivants*.'[5] The kinds of identity politics discussed in this book count on and count with a certain concept of democracy to further their emancipatory ideals. The rhetoric of equal rights and freedom from oppression has recourse to a presumed *determinable* conception of democracy and it is on this basis that identity movements calculate.[6] The challenges that identity politics have raised to the universality of Man as the subject of liberty – an issue marked in both Chapters Two and Three – have produced re-interpretations and re-inscriptions of the subject as a calculative means to further the emancipatory promise. But as we have seen, the self-protection of the emancipatory subject has long been showing signs of its own undoing. Class struggle, which challenged the progress of humanity based on the bourgeois subject, underwent further re-inscriptions through challenges posed by the categories of sex, race/ethnicity, sexuality, and – as is all too familiar within identity politics – innumerable other categories of subjugated identities. The unmanageability and incompleteness of a list of subjugated identities indicates just how extended the process of self-division can keep multiplying as a means for maintaining some semblance of an emancipatory promise *for all* (as if it is decidable in advance who and what to include and exclude in a definition of 'all'). The signs of such calculation reaching a certain point of exhaustion currently trouble many proponents of identity politics, who mostly read the problems of the 'add and stir' approach to forming a more all-encompassing emancipatory subject as an impasse they have to overcome.[7] For Derrida, the impasse, or to use his term, the aporia cannot be overcome. Rather,

---

    5   J. Derrida, *Politics of Friendship*, trans. G. Collins (London, Verso, 1997), p. x.

    6   For example, see I. M. Young, *Inclusion and Democracy* (Oxford: Oxford University Press, 2002).

    7   This view is held by post-postivist realists discussed throughout this book. Also see S. Walby, 'Complexity Theory, Systems Theory and Multiple Intersecting Social Inequalities', *Philosophy of the Social Sciences*, 37, 4 (2007): 449–70. My thanks to Kerreen Reiger for bringing my attention to this article.

it is only after reaching such a point of exhaustion that new thinking and novel approaches to the elaboration of the emancipatory promise can begin otherwise.

The order of calculability must ineluctably negotiate with that which is beyond calculation. However, as ought to be clear from the previous chapter, to push identity politics beyond the order of the calculable – most often associated with, but not restricted to, legal struggles – does not mean that there is no need to calculate. As Derrida notes:

> Each advance in politicization obliges one to reconsider, and so to reinterpret the very foundations of law such as they had previously been calculated or delimited. This was true for example in the Declaration of the rights of Man, in the abolition of slavery, in all the emancipatory battles that remain and will have to remain in progress, everywhere in the world, for men and for women. *Nothing seems to me less outdated than the classical emancipatory ideal.* We cannot attempt to disqualify it today, whether crudely or with sophistication, at least not without treating it too lightly and forming the worst complicities.[8]

But the promise, as Derrida demonstrates, cannot and must not solely belong to the order of calculability; the promise is refractory to presence.[9] This is to say, the promise cannot arrive: to fulfil a promise would be to annul it, as there would no longer remain anything to fulfil. Of course, this does not mean that we therefore disregard the promise, as an oppositional logic might suggest. On the contrary, the structure of the promise must always contain an opening for *continual renewal* in order to remain as a promise. This opening, which must remain in disjointure, is what structures the promise for democracy as always 'to come'.

Between the calculability and incalculability of a democracy to come

Without renouncing the concept of democracy, Derrida questions the way in which political movements elaborate the promise for emancipation as if democracy is *presentable* (for identity politics is not alone in this). To proceed as if such movements know what democracy *is* and as if democracy knows who or what will arrive as other in its interminable task toward perfection would be to neglect the task of choosing and responding to a heritage that cannot be transparently given *within a known horizon*. This now familiar Derridean engagement with choosing a heritage and the impossibility of any concept being given over to the present has a particularly striking resonance when read against the inherited concept of democracy. As Derrida explains, the inherited concept of democracy welcomes contestation and the task of indefinitely improving itself, which is why democracy as 'a political experience of the impossible' has a better chance of welcoming the other than other political regimes contemplated in Plato's *Republic*.[10] To elaborate:

---

8 Derrida, 'Force of Law', p. 28, emphasis added.

9 Derrida, *Specters of Marx*.

10 Derrida, *Rogues: Two Essays on Reason*, pp. 21–7. As Plato discusses in the *Republic*, democracy, is not quite a 'regime'. Derrida considers Plato's misgivings about democracy in book 8 of *The Republic*. Plato fears that taking leadership in turns in democracy leaves leaders

Democracy is the only system, the only constitutional paradigm in which, in principle, one has or one takes the right to publicly criticise everything, including the idea of democracy, its concept, its history and its name. Including the idea of the constitutional paradigm and the absolute authority of law. It is therefore alone in being universalisable, and from this comes its chance and its fragility.[11]

The chance for and fragility of the emancipatory promise, which we have followed from the liberatory injunction marked in both the spirit of the Enlightenment and Marxism in Chapter Three, are inscribed *together*. There is no way of separating chance from threat that inheres in the fragility of the opening to the other or to the promise of a 'democracy to come'. And this is what has troubled and continues to trouble thinkers who want to ontologise or actualise the emancipatory promise. This was certainly the response from many left critics seeking to 'reconcile' their own inheritance to Marxism when Derrida attached a certain spirit of Marxism to the 'democracy to come'.[12]

A promise without content

Ernesto Laclau, for example, finds it problematic that Derrida defends a classic notion of emancipation at the same time in which the latter deconstructs the grounding of the contents in which the emancipatory promise 'crystallises'.[13] Laclau supposes that if the contents of the emancipatory promise cannot be grounded through an eschatological or teleological articulation – which Derrida demonstrates in *Specters of Marx* that it cannot – then the '"ontological" condition' of the promise remains indifferent to its contents. While Laclau's critique appears to take into account the logic of spectrality inhering in Derrida's pledge to the emancipatory promise through recognising Derrida's 'politics' without a *telos*, the former couches his critique with recourse to a politics of actuality. In other words, Laclau fails to situate the promise *between* the quasi-oppositions of the actual and ideal, whose conditions of (im)possibility are accounted for through the logic of the spectral and hauntological. Laclau cannot help but seek a way of ontologising the promise in wanting to actualise its contents. Consequently, he looks for a way to 'supersede' what he sees as 'the ambiguity ... between undecidability as a terrain of radicalisation of the decision and undecidability as the source of an ethical injunction'.[14] As indicated earlier, this is not an uncommon response to deconstructive writing from those engaged with emancipatory politics. The fear is that by remaining open to the unidentifiable other, deconstruction cannot stand opposed to any form of exclusion. For Laclau, the opening to the other cannot exclude the possibility of the promise becoming occupied,

---

with weak authority. While Plato finds this form of government threatening, Derrida sees such a threat as also a chance.

11 Derrida, *Rogues: Two Essays on Reason*, p. 87.

12 Responses to Derrida's *Specters of Marx* are collected in the anthology edited by M. Sprinker, *Ghostly Demarcations: A Symposium on Jacques Derrida's 'Specters of Marx'* (London and New York: Verso, 1999).

13 E. Laclau, 'The Time is out of Joint', *Diacritics*, 25, 2 (1995): 86–96.

14 Ibid., p. 95.

for instance, by totalitarian contents. As he puts it, 'a case for totalitarianism can be presented starting from deconstructionist premises'.[15] But as argued in Chapter Three, in relation to the inheritance of Marxism's spectres, totalitarianism may emerge from Marxist premises. This is also true for any form of identity politics. The name of feminism can be used for anti-feminist purposes, anti-racist premises can be appropriated toward racist ends, as can anti-homophobic platforms be turned toward homophobic practices. Of course, the list could be multiplied. What all such movements share in common is *a division within identity from the beginning*, a non-negotiable complicity with a faulty writing – the impossible, yet necessary, language of ontology – which is indispensable for such movements to acquire legibility, intelligibility and communicability.

In his critique of the promise, Laclau shares with other critics attempting to overcome the 'impasses' of deconstruction, the failure to follow through the implications of working with the non-negotiable complicity that conditions the (im)possibility of presence between any two oppositional predicates. Instead, as previously mentioned, he proceeds as if he were working in a space of pure oppositional logic. This is further demonstrated with what he deduces from the idea that the 'non-connection between structural undecidability and ethical injunction' can lead to the proposition that 'openness to the heterogeneity of the other is an ethical injunction' itself. He states: 'If one takes this proposition at face value, one is forced to conclude that we have to accept the other as different because she is different, whatever the content of that heterogeneity would be.'[16] What Laclau fails to do here is situate the ethical injunction in relation to the aporias of justice, where the making of a decision is far from an indifferent process. Caputo (albeit in another context) explains the problem of aligning deconstruction with an indiscriminate predisposition to the excluded and marginal:

> The mistake here is to construe deconstruction in an excessively formal sense and to pay no attention to the substantive merits of what is in or out of power, i.e, to whether or not forces that are in power are just forces. For deconstruction 'is' justice and Derrida says (almost) that he knows of nothing more just – and he should know. Exclusion and marginalization, thus, are never merely formal ideas; they always have to do with damaged lives and disasters.[17]

Far from encouraging an indifference to the contents of the emancipatory promise, deconstruction shows an interminable commitment to attend to the *singular* cases – 'little proper names', as Caputo might say – that exceed any determined contents of the emancipatory ideal. The *finite* and fragile call from the other *is not anticipatable* within any *determined* concept of democracy, and that is why Derrida negotiates with the risk of disjointure and non-gathering, and why he refuses to situate the coming of democracy as an 'event' that will arrive in the present. As will be argued below, if we know the content, to use Laclau's word, of the other's 'identity' then we not only place a condition on democracy's hospitality, but close the opening

---

15 Ibid., p. 93.
16 Ibid.
17 Caputo, *Against Ethics*, p. 119.

to democracy's interminable task of improving itself and welcoming the other. In the terms of the previous chapter, the aporia between the universalised calculability of law and the incalculable singularity of justice inscribed within the promise of democracy, therefore 'must always risk being perverted into a threat'.[18]

The aporetic injunctions of democracy

On one side of the aporia, democracy pledges itself to the injunction that requires 'the universality of rational calculation, of the equality of citizens before the law, the social bond of being together'.[19] This side of democracy lends itself to the rhetoric of government policy, to the calculated vernacular of 'national interest' and citizen restraint for the cause of the greater good, and protection of the state's sovereignty – measures whose empirical manifestations in the world today are far from any democratic ideal. Post Cold War claims that the emancipatory promise of democracy is inhabited in the form of free market capitalism that drives the United States economy, simply fail to measure up as a marker of freedom and equality, even in its own terms. As occupying the hegemonic articulation of democracy tied to the sovereignty of particular nation states, this calculated version of the democratic easily loses sight of the finite and fragile calls of singular others that approach democracy from the other side of the aporia. The other side of the aporia must remain open to the 'incalculable singularity of *any one*, before any "subject", the possible undoing of the social bond by a secret to be respected, beyond all citizenship, beyond every "state", indeed every "people," indeed beyond the current state of the definition of a living being as living "human" being'. So once again, there is the impossible, where the aporetic relation remains ineffaceable – for which we must remain vigilant – and where the impossible beckons us to respond. To demonstrate how the aporia operates in a specific context, I will look at how the nominal democracy of Australia negotiates its sovereignty in the face of those others who knock on Australia's door as non-citizens and ask for refuge.

Sovereignty and autoimmunity in Australia's 'democracy'

One side of the aporia, the order of calculability – that informs struggles for equality of citizens before the law – must have recourse to sovereign identity. Democracy, Derrida contends, inherits a tradition that remains unthinkable without recourse to sovereignty. Michael Naas considers this point in relation to sovereign subjectivity as he ponders the meanings of 'auto- prefixed words' – *auto*nomous, *auto*mobilic, *auto*telic, for examples – before describing Derrida's work on the *auto*immunity of democracy.[20] Autoimmunity is the only *autos* word that does *not* express 'power, independence, and stability of an enduring self'. The democratic ideal of freedom

---

18 Derrida, 'Autoimmunity: Real and Symbolic Suicides', p. 120.

19 Ibid. All quotations from this paragraph are from the same page. Emphasis added.

20 M. Naas, '"One Nation … Indivisible": Jacques Derrida on the Autoimmunity of Democracy and Sovereignty of God', *Research in Phenomenology*, 36 (2006): 15–44.

depends on a notion of sovereignty that is 'grounded in the *autos*'. The *autos* grounds

> ... the self or the selfsame, in the sovereignty of self-positioning, self-asserting, and [a] deciding self that has the capacity in and of itself to choose something for itself, to vote one way or another by itself, to affirm or deny from out of itself in order to sustain itself and assert its sovereignty as a self. There would be no freedom, no freedom to choose, to vote, to assemble, to speak, to pledge allegiance, without the notion of a selfsame self that does the choosing, the voting, or the speaking, that is, without the authority or capacity of some sovereign self.[21]

Derrida uses the term *ipseity* to refer to the self that gives itself its own law, encapsulating the power of an "I can".[22] This idea of the sovereign self is thought through 'the turn and return', upon the 'self of an origin', which Derrida juxtaposes to the turns of a 'quasi-circular' rotation that also propels the space of a 'democracy to come'. In this space, taking turns – through 'the alternating form of *by turns*, the *in turn*, the *each in turn*'[23] – for governing the people, conditions the sovereignty of the people as a nation, which *attempts* to gather and keep gathering to itself the assemblage of what we colloquially call 'living together'. To put the term of *ipseity* to work in the face of a 'democracy to come', Derrida asks, 'what is "living together?"' He continues, 'must one live together only with one's like?'[24] Whether asked in terms of the sovereign self or the sovereign people in the form of a nation state that calls itself democratic, the question turns upon the logic of the same principle of ipseity, and so each can analogously take turns in explicating the *force* or power that lies at the heart of a self-legitimating sovereignty. So how does Australia's self-legitimating sovereignty negotiate 'living together' as a democratic nation?

Australian sovereignty and 'border protection'

The Commonwealth of Australia was established in 1901, forming a federation from six British colonies that became states of the nation. The very first enactments of legislation passed in parliament included the expulsion of thousands of indentured labourers that were brought from the Pacific Islands to work in sugar cane fields in Queensland[25] and the infamous *Immigration Restriction Act 1901*.[26] More commonly

---

21 Ibid., p. 19.

22 Derrida, *Rogues*, p. 10. Derrida notes the Latin *ipse* translates to the Greek *autos*, p. 12.

23 Ibid., p. 13.

24 Ibid., p. 11.

25 For a detailed and incisive account of Pacific Islander indentured labour see T. Banivanua-Mar, *Violence and Colonial Dialogue: The Australian-Pacific Indentured Labor Trade* (Honolulu: University of Hawaii Press, 2007).

26 Of course, the various colonies before federation all had their own forms of immigration restrictions. Federation formalised, however, the identification with a British heritage, setting the agenda to form a White Australia. See A. Markus, 'Of Continuities and Discontinuities: Reflections on a Century of Australian Immigration Control', in L. Jayasuriya, D. Walker and

known as the White Australia Policy – a policy that underwent several mutations over the years, but whose loose ends remained until around the early 1970s – the legislation aimed at excluding all non-Europeans from immigrating into Australian shores. The building of a White nation, of course depended on effacing its original inhabitants. The opening of the Commonwealth of Australia made only two references to Aboriginal people in federal legislation. First, that Aboriginal people were to be excluded from the Australian census (an exclusion that remained until 1967, when a national referendum overwhelmingly voted 'yes' to include Aboriginal people in the census count).[27] And second, the federal parliament legislated to allow each state to retain their own version of their already existing Aborigines Protection Act, as the Government evidently thought that Aboriginal people were a dying race and could be better regulated in the meantime on a state level.[28] The various Protection Acts allowed states to regulate the lives of Aboriginal people through placing restrictions on where and under what conditions Aboriginal people could live and work, who they could marry, who they could socialise with and where they could socialise, among other daily practices. As discussed in the previous chapter, these Protection Acts included the power to remove children from their families.

Might makes right – Australia's refugee policy

It would be naïve to think that the objective to build a White Nation was dead and buried with a government change of policy just as it would be naïve to think that there were no counter narratives to White Australia when the past policy was operative.[29] The spectres of both White supremacy and multicultural diversity continue to compete with one another in a nation where the status between host and stranger remains unsettled. The founding of Australia's sovereignty overtly carries the force of exclusionary practices. At the same time, the specific instituting act of founding this nation exposes the structure for *any* founding act of law more generally – that

---

J. Gothard (eds), *Legacies of White Australia* (Perth: University of Western Australia Press, 2003), pp. 175–89. For an account of how the White Australia Policy is situated in a global context, see Chapter 6 in M. Lake and H. Reynolds, *Drawing the Global Colour Line: White Men's Countries and the Question of Racial Equality* (Melbourne: Melbourne University Press, 2008), pp. 137–65.

27 For an account of the discrepancies between the way the referendum of 1967 is represented in public discourse and the actual legislation that was passed see B. Attwood and A. Markus, *The 1967 Referendum: Race, Power and the Australian Constitution* (Canberra: Aboriginal Studies Press, 2007).

28 As each state had varying legislation, and various amendments at different times, it is difficult to form a singular chart of each Aborigines Protection Act. An idea of variations in legislation from state to state can be gleaned from a table drawn up by Anna Haebich that charts the legislation and institutions concerning 'Protections of Aborigines' with regard to Aboriginal children in particular. See A. Haebich, *Broken Circles: Fragmenting Indigenous Families 1800–2000* (Fremantle: Arts Press, 2001). The table is found on pp.149–50. The book has a particular emphasis on Western Australia.

29 See C. Elder, *Being Australian: Narratives of National Identity* (Sydney: Allen and Unwin, 2007).

the authority of law founds its own legitimacy in the very act of instituting itself. The founding of Australia as a nation, however, offers a particularly illustrative example where law clearly sides with the English saying that 'might makes right' – a phrase which is the rough equivalent of the French '*La rasion du plus fort est toujours la meilleure*'.[30] These are the opening lines to the fable, 'The Wolf and the Lamb', which is cited in full before the Preface to *Rogues*. The English translation of the fable in *Rogues*, opens with 'The strong are always the best at proving they are right'. Once again, Derrida invites us to consider relations between force and law, and once again poses the question of whether justice would be reducible to law. Raising the question of law (*droit*) as rights (*droits*) in the context of Australia – where the question of *what* self-legitimating sovereignty, or *who* as a sovereign subject, can assert rights – exposes concretely the inherent contradictions contained within the concepts of sovereignty and ipseity more generally.

Australia's articulation of its self-identity is a constant source of anxiety on both a national and international level. Such anxiety over national sovereignty trickles all the way down to the self-identity of particular Australian citizens as sovereign subjects. There are numerous examples in Australia's past and present that could illustrate the point, but given the context of calculating with democracy, I will focus on one whose expression aired in the form of an electorate. When Pauline Hanson from the One Nation Party gained a seat in Parliament in the federal election of 1996, there was an astounding ease in which the spectre of the anti-Chinese panic of 1880s – a panic informing the *Immigration Restriction Act, 1901* – reappeared in the form of an 'Asian invasion' complex. In her maiden speech in parliament, Hanson asserted Australia's geographical location in a region of Asian populations posed a constant threat not only to Australian sovereignty, but also to Australian citizens who were being 'swamped by Asians' in the market for employment as well as lifestyle. (In Hanson's words, 'They have their own culture and religion, they form ghettos and do not assimilate.'[31]) The Australian Labor Party did not predict the appeal One Nation policies would have with many of their own blue collar voters, while the conservative Liberal and National Parties, who formed the Coalition Government, jumped on the populist bandwagon to denounce minority groups and multicultural policies as outmoded forms of 'political correctness'. In the years to follow, Hanson's policies remained popular amongst a significant proportion of the electorate despite her own political demise. Indeed, the previous Federal Government successfully adopted and absorbed much of One Nation's principles into mainstream policy during their term in office. Nowhere was this clearer than in the development of Australia's refugee policy.

In 2001, one hundred years after the first Australian parliament passed the *Immigration Restriction Act*, the Government introduced the *Border Protection Act* and the *Migration Amendment (Excision from Migration Zone) Act*. How did the expression '*border protection*' come to represent Australia's response to those

---

30 M. Naas, translates this 'La rasion du plus fort' as 'The reason of the strongest', *Rogues* p. 161n1. We can fill in the rest as, 'is always the best'.

31 Relevant extracts from Pauline Hanson's maiden speech in Federal Parliament can be accessed at http://www.multiculturalaustralia.edu.au/doc/hanson_1.pdf.

seeking asylum? The rapidity in which the aforementioned legislation was drafted and passed through parliament was extraordinary. The Government prevented boats entering Australian waters by excising Indian Ocean island territories from Australia's migration zone – these legislative changes were a direct intervention and response to what is famously known as the *Tampa* crisis.[32] MV *Tampa* was the name of the Norwegian tanker that rescued a sinking boat carrying 438 asylum seekers, who were mostly Hazaras from Afghanistan fleeing from the Taliban. While Australia's maritime authorities had issued an alert that there was a boat in distress, the Australian Government refused to allow Captain Arne Rinnan of the MV *Tampa* to enter Australian Territory. With sick and distressed people on a vessel licensed to carry only 50 passengers, Captain Rinnan entered Australian waters anyway, only to be stopped four miles from Christmas Island, where the military intervened and transferred the asylum seekers onto the naval frigate, HMAS *Manoora*. The asylum seekers were eventually taken to Nauru, whose government received tens of millions of dollars in exchange for housing a detention centre until refugee status was processed. No time limit was placed on processing applications for asylum. In its report on Australia's detention system in 2002, a delegation from the United Nations Human Rights Committee stated, 'to the knowledge of the delegation, a system combining mandatory, automatic, indiscriminate and indefinite detention without real access to court challenge is not practised by any other country in the world'.[33]

Public opinion at that time, according to opinion polls and confirmed by the Coalition's return to Government in 2001, favoured the Howard Government's stance when he announced, 'I yield to nobody in my determination to maintain the absolute right of Australia to decide who comes here and the circumstances in which they come'.[34] Consider the resonance of Howard's statement with that made in Hanson's first speech in parliament: 'If I can invite whom I want into my home, then I should have the right to have a say in who comes into my country'.[35] Howard uttered his statement in 2001, five years after Hanson's speech, and just over two weeks after 'September 11'. The terrorist attacks of 'September 11' were sandwiched between the beginning of the *Tampa* crisis on 26 August, and the Royal Assent of the 'border protection' legislation on 29 September that ushered in the so-called 'Pacific solution'. What is less well known, or what became obfuscated from public view, is that Justice North had ruled in the Federal Court – with reference to the principle of *habeas corpus*, which prohibits detention without legal reason – that the refugees who had boarded the *Tampa* should be granted asylum. His decision was handed

---

32 For a more detailed account of the Tampa Crisis see R. Manne with D. Corlett, *Sending Them Home: Refugees and the New Politics of Indifference*, Quarterly Essay 13 (Melbourne: Black Inc., 2004) and R. Manne, 'The Road to Tampa', in L. Jayasuriya, D. Walker and J. Gothard (eds), *Legacies of White Australia* (Perth: University of Western Australia Press, 2003), pp. 163–94.

33 Cited in J. Burnside, *Watching Brief: Reflections on Human Rights, Law and Justice* (Melbourne: Scribe, 2007), p. 121.

34 J. Howard, National Press Club, Canberra, 8/11/2001 http://sievx.com/articles/disaster/20011108JohnHoward.html accessed 23/11/07.

35 See footnote 31.

down only nine hours before the attacks on the Twin Towers.[36] When Justice North's decision was overturned three weeks later, the plight of asylum seekers had somehow become wedded to discourses around 'terrorism' such that media and Government references to 'illegals' and 'boat people' became more or less synonymous with 'terrorists', who allegedly warranted a need to maintain the safety and security of Australian borders. The newly articulated 'war against terror', allowed an assertion of Australian sovereignty that manufactured hostility rather than hospitality toward those most in need of it.

The paradox between sovereignty and democracy – the autoimmune process

When a nation state like Australia asserts sovereignty in such a way that it immunises itself from all other competing spectres fighting over its heritage and promise for a future, it does so in an undemocratic manner. In this way, the nation state is fighting against its own democracy – and so both democracy and sovereignty are inseparably and contradictorily caught within a process of autoimmunisation with one another. Yet it is not a simple case of resolving the contradiction. Relations between democracy and sovereignty are paradoxical. Derrida explains the paradox in the context of the UN Security Council, but the point is equally valid for Australia's sovereignty as a nation state:

> For democracy to be effective, for it to give rise to a system of law that can carry the day, which is to say, for it to give rise to an effective power, the *cracy* of the *dēmos* … is required. What is required is thus a sovereignty, a force that is stronger than all other forces in the world [or in the case of a nation state, the constituencies of the nation]. But if the constitution of this force is, in principle, supposed to represent and protect this world democracy[or nation in this case], it in fact betrays and threatens it from the very outset in an autoimmune fashion, and in a way that is … just as silent as it is unavowable.[37]

How is this so? First, by definition, for sovereignty to be sovereign it must be indivisible. Derrida affirms Carl Schmitt's recognition that the 'decisionist exceptionality' accorded to sovereignty can be so only because by definition sovereignty cannot be shared. As such, sovereignty is excluded in principle from time and language as 'the act of sovereignty must and can, by force, put an end in a single, indivisible stroke to the endless discussion' that is associated with debating and deliberation that defines a democracy.[38] The silent force of sovereignty is what lends itself to its deciding exceptionality, which sets in motion the autoimmune process in democracy. Derrida offers two examples to demonstrate the autoimmunity of democracy through the exceptional decision. The first involves the suspension of elections in Algeria in 1992, when it became evident that a majority vote would select a party that would put an end to democracy by installing itself as a theocratic state. The second example concerns the imposition of laws and constraints on

---

36 Burnside, *Watching Brief*, p. 106.
37 Derrida, *Rogues*, p. 100.
38 Ibid., pp. 9–10. citation, p. 10.

citizenry freedom within the United States of America post September 11. Both examples involve an exception to democratic principles in the name of protecting and immunising democracy from what appears as a greater threat to the very *life* of democracy. Both cases are quite different, underscoring the necessity not to declare hastily that the autoimmune process is inherently good or bad. For whether the process of autoimmunity protects or perverts the emancipatory promise is not straightforwardly decidable, and the rhetoric of protecting oneself in order to thwart a greater threat to the principles of democracy can too readily provide an excuse for the worst kind of abuse of power. For example, the rhetoric of self-protection propels the logic that has allowed Australia to develop such an austere and heartless refugee policy. Each case of the aforementioned autoimmune process is singular, where judgement over whether the promise is protected or perverted is different each time. Yet, there is a structural similarity insofar as each case involves the sovereign power of making an exceptional decision.[39] In allowing itself the exceptional decision, the 'democratic' nation state asserts its sovereignty without necessarily having the backing of the populace.

In enacting an exceptional decision, the sovereign state demonstrates that the 'reason of the strongest' is strongest precisely because it does not have to give reasons. For to give a reason, or to justify one's sovereignty, is to enter language and a code of law that divides the authority of the sovereign. In other words, the universalising medium that is necessary for me to speak to the other, the universalisable law that is necessary for a suprasovereignty to facilitate and mediate an association of nations, or the universalising law necessary for the people to recognise the sovereign nation state as democratic, all betray the ipseity of the One that defines sovereignty. Thus, the universalising imperative for a democracy is incompatible with sovereignty, even though, as cited above, the force of sovereignty is required to make democracy effective. This paradox is at the heart of what turns sovereignty and democracy against one another and against themselves.

> To confer sense or meaning on sovereignty, to justify it, … is thus to divide it … to compromise its immunity. This happens as soon as one speaks of it in order to give it or find in it some sense or meaning. But since this happens all the time, pure sovereignty does not exist; it is always in the process of positing itself by refuting itself, by denying or disavowing itself; it is always in the process of autoimmunizing itself, or betraying itself by betraying the democracy that nonetheless can never do without it.[40]

It should not be surprising that the purity of sovereignty as indivisible is contaminated from the moment we seek to confer meaning on it. For both the sovereign self and the sovereign state are *finite* entities located in the muddle of concrete history, which is *between* past and future, between the living and the dead, but always caught within

---

39 Giorgio Agamben argues that this state of exception, supposedly a provisional measure, has now become a normalized paradigm of government. See G. Agamben, *State of Exception*, trans. K. Attell (Chicago, IL: University of Chicago Press, 2005); and *Homo Sacer: Sovereign Power and Bare Life*, trans. D. Heller Roazen (Stanford, CA: Stanford University Press, 1998).

40 Ibid., p. 101.

the hyperbolic web of spectrality in order to acquire intelligibility. The self-identity of any sovereignty, whether in the form of a communist or democratic state or the subject of any identity movement, is therefore always caught between oppositional predicates such as life and death, absence and presence. Citing immunologist, Edward Golub, Donna Haraway astutely observes, 'the immune system must recognize *self* in some manner in order to react to something foreign'.[41] The autoimmune process is set in motion when the self has trouble distinguishing itself from something foreign. In this process of autoimmunity '"self" and "other" lose their rationalistic oppositional quality'.[42] But it is not as if self and other were discrete from one another to begin with. As Derrida notes of the logic of spectrality, 'What happens between the two, and between all the "two's" one likes, such as between life and death, can only maintain itself with some ghost.'[43] As argued in Chapter Three, the 'living ego' and the material structures in need of practical transformation – such as the state – that Marx opposed to the dead and the domain of ideal representation, cannot do without 'the relative autonomy of ghostly reality'. The logic of the spectre is necessary to render the materiality of the ego, the state and the church intelligible to know *how* to work upon *what* material structures that need transformation. Marx's failure to learn to live with ghosts and the spectral that he so adamantly sought to put to death – in commanding the spectre of communism to actualise – is also a failure to come to terms with the autoimmune process. Derrida's reading of Marx's reading of Stirner offers, as other commentators like Naas have noted, an earlier introduction to the autoimmune process.

> They both share, apparently like you and me, an unconditional preference for the living body. But precisely because of that, they wage an endless war against whatever represents it, whatever is not the body but belongs to it: prosthesis and delegation, repetition, différance. The living ego is autoimmune [*Le moi vivant est auto-immune*], which is what they do not want to know. To protect its life, to constitute itself as unique living ego, to relate, as the same, to itself, it is necessarily led to welcome the other within (so many figures of death: différance of the technical apparatus, iterability, non-uniqueness, prosthesis, synthetic image, simulacrum, all of which begins with language, before language), it must therefore take the immune defenses apparently meant for the non-ego, the enemy, the opposite, the adversary and direct them at once *for itself and against itself*.[44]

Once again, the impossibility of self-presence as *différance* reveals a fracture, an opening to the other that is *within* the movement of identification, not outside. Thus the autoimmune process is also a critique of self-presence. Autoimmunity consists

---

41 D. Haraway, 'The Biopolitics of Postmodern Bodies: Constitutions of Self in Immune System Discourse', in *Simians, Cyborgs and Women: The Reinvention of Nature* (London: Free Association Books, 1991), pp. 203–30. This citation, p. 230. Haraway uses the autoimmune process to consider new ways of thinking self and other for an oppositional politics. She states, 'My thesis is that the immune system is an elaborate icon for principal systems of symbolic and material "difference" in late capitalism' (p. 204). Her essay was first delivered as a conference paper in 1988.

42 Ibid., p. 218.

43 Derrida, *Specters*, p. xviii.

44 Ibid., p. 141.

not only of 'destroying one's own protections' in the life of a presumed sovereign identity, but compromises ipseity itself. As Naas puts it, autoimmunity compromises 'the *autos* itself as the foundation and guarantor of identity'. It is precisely the lack of self-identity that makes democracy autoimmune, and more amenable to rethinking sovereignty. Whether in the form of the Security Council of the United Nations, the superpower of the United States of America, or a lesser member of the 'coalition of the willing' such as Australia, each sovereign entity is compromised, or must compromise itself in an autoimmune fashion in order to respect the universalising principle built into the inheritance of democracy. The same principle applies to any identity movement. For the principle of democracy is to give power to the people, which means to push sovereignty beyond its own definition of indivisibility – to invent 'new divisions of sovereignty' that will extend itself beyond nation-state sovereignty and beyond citizenship. This imagining leads to the other side of the aporia, already inscribed within the principle of democracy – the democratic principle that welcomes the 'incalculable singularity of *any one*'. This could be the figure of the foreigner, or someone or something completely other. First, let's examine the face-to-face encounter with the foreigner as refugee.

Hosting the stranger in Australia

Conditional hospitality

Sometimes the foreigner as refugee arrives as a single person, perhaps fleeing from fear of persecution due to sexual orientation, for example. But mostly and increasingly today, refugees fleeing from persecution are numbered in the hundreds, thousands and millions.[45] In an attempt not to undermine the singularity of any one, Derrida states, that 'to cite the best known [example of a particular refugee] would risk sending the anonymous others back into the darkness (*mal*) from which they find it hard to escape, a darkness which is truly the worst and the condition of all others'.[46] In this instance, refraining from naming the singularity of the one who calls for justice is to accentuate that all the anonymous others are also singular incoming calls that are each finite and fragile. Yet, writing in Australia, some names have garnered more attention than others for highlighting the sheer ineptness of the rule of law being able to cope with the call for justice. Still, remaining open to the singularity of each call, whilst seeking ways to deal with the massive influx of such calls in a language that compromises the singularity of each other, is what calls

---

45 Of course, statistics depend on definitions. The UNHCR estimates that by the end of 2006 there were about 9.9 million refugees worldwide and 32.9 million persons of concern. However, the UNHCR also notes that 4.3 million Palestinian refugees are not detailed in their report because they fall under the United Nations Relief and Works Agency for Palestinian Refugees in the Near East. The numbers, to me, are incomprehensible. See UNHCR 'Global Trends 2006: Refugees, Asylum Seekers, Returnees, Internally Displaced and Stateless Persons', Division of Operational Services, July 2007. http://www.unhcr.org/statistics/STATISTICS/4676a71d4.pdf.

46 Derrida, *Cosmopolitanism and Forgiveness*, p. 6.

for response within the entire contents of this book – investigations concerning the entangled relations between politics, ontology and ethics – in its pledge to further the emancipatory promise.

The book began by questioning the protocol to declare one's identity before speaking only to reach the figure of the refugee where the speaking subject has no means to verify his or her identity. While inscriptions of identity no doubt play a role in the formation of a refugee's status, the refugee most often arrives in a foreign land with no documented proof of that identity (national, ethnic, political, religious or otherwise). Without identity papers, the foreigner/stranger knocks upon the door of a sovereign state like Australia, with a dire need for refuge. In Levinasian terms, the refugee asks for asylum without anything but the nakedness of her face. Does the 'host' offer hospitality without condition? Or must the foreigner meet a number of conditions before hospitality is even considered? How to turn the seemingly opposing two poles of hospitality to work otherwise than through an either/or logic?

Notwithstanding the tenuous division between host and stranger that sits at the foundation of Australia as a sovereign nation state, the division between citizen and non-citizen currently informs and produces inhospitable policies concerning the rights of refugees. Australia's record of detaining 'unlawful non-citizens', underscores the rupture between law and justice in a context where discourses (in the Foucauldian sense) on human rights of refugees are compelled to negotiate with the calculable domains of national and international law.[47] Hannah Arendt noted the difficulty over fifty years ago, which many contemporary thinkers cite for its pertinence today. She states, 'The conception of human rights, based upon the assumed existence of a human being as such, broke down at the very moment when those who professed to believe in it were for the first time confronted with people who had indeed lost all other qualities and specific relationships – except that they were human.'[48] This peculiar predicament challenges discourses of human rights through the figure of the refugee, which has particular relevance for current articulations of identity movements more generally. I will return to this. The immediate task is to shift from the calculable domain of policy to the incalculable order of justice and ethics.

As Toula Nicolacopoulos and George Vassilacopoulos point out, much discussion about Australia's treatment of refugees is 'typically framed' in terms of 'competing international humanitarian and national interests'.[49] To put this in terms of the

---

47 One of the more notorious cases where the classification of an 'unlawful non-citizen' perpetuated unnecessary detention involved Al Kateb, a person who was born stateless in Kuwait as the son of Palestinian refugees from Gaza. In 2004, the High court ruled that the Immigration Minister had the right to indefinitely detain Kateb, because he could not be deported. In 2007, Kateb was finally granted permission to reside in Australia indefinitely. See D. Marr, 'Escape from Life in Limbo', *Sydney Morning Herald*, 27 October 2007. http://www.smh.com.au/news/national/escape-from-a-life-in-limbo/2007/10/26/1192941339538.html.

48 H. Arendt, *The Origins of Totalitarianism* (New York: Harcourt, Brace Jovanovich, 1979), p. 299. This point is cited by Derrida in *Cosmopolitanism and Forgivenss*, and Agamben, *Means Without End*.

49 T. Nicolacopoulos and George Vassilacopoulos, 'On the Other side of Xenophobia: Philoxenia as the Ground of Refugee Rights', *Australian Journal of Human Rights*, 17 (2004),

preceding discussion of the chapter, such a framing involves calculations between a sovereign nation state, and a suprasovereignty that supposedly presides over the protection of human rights of its national signatories. Powerful and compassionate commentaries on Australia's refugee policy by Robert Manne and Julian Burnside, for instance, have brought to public attention the breaches of Australia's humanitarian obligations under international law, specifically, breaches under the International Covenant on Civil and Political Rights, the Convention against Torture, and the Convention on the Rights of the Child. Since the *Tampa* crisis, an increasing number of lawyers, journalists, community activist groups, individual citizens and even backbenchers of the previous Federal Government's own party have operated within the same calculable framework of calling Australia's refugee policy into account. In the meantime, detention centres such as Baxter and Woomera – two of the most geographically remote, and most notorious for their harsh treatment of refugees – have been closed. Still, there have been no substantial changes in Australia's mandatory detention policy. It is still lawful to detain refugees indefinitely within Australia. As the new Federal Government takes its turn in leading the nation, it pays to remember that mandatory detention was first introduced in 1992, when the Australian Labor Party were in office. It bears repeating that there is still the imperative to calculate as far as possible with law, politics, economics, psychiatry and all other institutional sites that condition Australia's approach to refugees. *But it is only through addressing the incalculable order of ethics and justice that the emancipatory promise can remain open and responsive to the unforeseeable interruption that the stranger/foreigner poses to current discourses on human rights.* Nicolacopoulos and Vassilacopoulos join an increasing number of commentators that follow Derrida in shifting focus from the order of calculable government policies, to reframe the approach to asylum seekers in terms of the incalculable dimension of 'unconditional hospitality'. This dimension is informed by Levinas's face-to-face relation.

Unconditional hospitality

As Derrida sees it, hospitality, like justice, '*is*' ethics. It makes no sense, therefore, to speak of an ethic of hospitality. Hospitality, justice and ethics all bear the movement and openness toward the other, marked in the present chapter through the phrase, *vers l'etranger*. It is not exactly accurate to substitute the terms stranger for foreigner, and each of these for the wholly other, but holding the three in tension with one another enables a more nuanced and stratified approach for considering how each different form of alterity disrupts the logic of identity based movements. In *Of Hospitality*, Derrida (or rather Derrida's English translator) opts for mostly referring to the foreigner. For Derrida the question of hospitality begins in the situation where the foreigner must ask for hospitality in the language of the host, which is other than his own. Derrida asks,

---

http://www.austlii.edu.au/au/journals/AJHR/2004/17.html. Philoxenia translates to love of the foreigner/stranger. The authors use the concept in conjunction with Derrida's unconditional hospitality to foster an ethic to 'act as if there were no borders'.

Must we ask the foreigner to understand us, to speak our language, in all the senses of this term, in all its possible extensions, before being able and so as to be able to welcome him into our country? If he was already speaking our language, with all that that implies, if we already shared everything that is shared with a language, would the foreigner still be a foreigner and could we speak of asylum or hospitality in regard to him? [50]

Derrida uses this paradox to contrast the foreigner as someone other – who is recognisable as someone with a name, a family, a language and a nation – with the absolute other who does not have a name or family name. The distinction forces a reckoning with the heterogeneity of two orders of hospitality as conditional and unconditional. Derrida points to a cosmopolitan tradition that recognises a 'pact' of hospitality that is due to the foreigner by right. In this tradition, to receive the foreigner, 'you begin by asking his name; you enjoin him to state and to guarantee his identity, as you would a witness in court'.[51] When the foreigner discloses his name, he becomes responsible before law and the host. As such the host maintains sovereignty over his home. It would be fair to say that this tradition currently informs national and international law regarding the processing of refugees, though as we have seen the administration of such processing is far from welcoming. Evidently, in Australia the condition of speaking the host language is often placed upon the foreigner – whether an asylum seeker or a business person from a non-English speaking background – before any welcome is granted.[52]

Derrida then turns to the question of whether the disclosure of name ought to be a condition of hospitality. For while it is customary to ask for a name from a stranger/foreigner in order to address her, this ought not to be the condition upon which you offer hospitality. While the stranger/foreigner is the one who knocks on my door to come into my home without invitation, I can unreservedly welcome the stranger only if I create the receptive and responsive conditions to keep my door open. I do not know who the stranger/foreigner is, and to offer my unconditional hospitality, I welcome her or him without asking for any disclosure or verification of identity. For my hospitality to remain pure, I must greet the other not out of civic or legal duty, or because I expect reciprocity, as this would reduce my hospitality to a calculable transaction that would kill the spirit of a genuine welcome. This idea of pure hospitality, particularly in the context of Australia's refugee policy, seems an impossible imperative. Yet, having heard already that deconstruction is driven by the impossible, we are better prepared to hear that the impossibility of unconditional hospitality is what provides the conditions of possibility to think through more just ways of dealing with the decisions and responsibilities governing hospitality in concrete practice. For it 'is the pure and hyperbolical hospitality in whose name one

---

50 Derrida, *Of Hospitality*, pp. 16–17.

51 Ibid., p. 29.

52 For an account of Derrida's reading of Kant's cosmopolitan tradition of hospitality in relation to how foreigners are treated with regard to Australian business visa requirements, see A. Kordvani, 'Hospitality, Politics of mobility, and Movement of Service Suppliers under the GATS', *Melbourne Journal of International Law*, 7 (2006): 74–103.

should always invent the best dispositions, the least bad conditions, the most just legislation, so as to make [hospitality] as effectively as possible'.[53]

While this principle of pure hospitality is constantly suspended or betrayed in practice it is nevertheless the law of unlimited hospitality that we try to create the best 'laws (in the plural)' for the reception of foreigners. The imposition of conditions on hospitality arises in order to maintain control of my home or status as host. In this situation, there is always the possibility that the stranger will threaten my position as host, by encroaching on the threshold of what makes my home mine. If the stranger occupies my home in such a way that it no longer feels like my home, and if this reaches a point where I feel that I am no longer playing host, then I am no longer in a position to offer hospitality. As Caputo describes the situation following Derrida's reference to Benveniste, 'there is always a little hostility in hospitality'. He notes that the etymological roots of the word 'hospitality' carry the word's opposite: 'The word "hospitality" derives from the Latin *hospes*, which is formed from *hostis*, which originally meant a "stranger" and came to take on the meaning of the enemy or "hostile" stranger (*hostilits*)'.[54] This etymological connection emphasises not only the demand that sovereignty of self is required in order to play host, but highlights how both conditional and unconditional hospitality can corrupt one another. As such relations between the two, like other oppositional pairs, are both irreducible and indissociable. The decision to offer hospitality remains between the abyss of each side of conditionality and unconditionality.

The stranger/foreigner and the wholly other

Reference to the foreigner is not substitutable with the wholly other, but in many ways the foreigner's relation to the host who offers hospitality allows another way for thinking justice as the disjuncture necessary for remaining open to what is coming. To put this in terms of the wholly other, as my relationship to the other is an unintentional consciousness that interrupts and accompanies my *bonne conscience* in its intentionality, I am in an ethical relation with the other *before* any thematisation or verification of the other's identity. I am at the receiving end of an injunction to take responsibility for the other's death. This situation of the other's death is the situation that has led the refugee to knock on my door. This could well be the knock from someone or something well beyond my anticipation. I will refuse to respond to the knock if I do not keep open the disjuncture necessary for the other to come. On the receiving end of the call, I am obligated to prevent the other's death before I ask the other to disclose her or his identity. Yet, within the logics and protocols of identity politics, disclosure is almost mandatory.

There is no doubt that proponents of identity politics would be sympathetic to the predicament of refugees, and the unreachable administrative demands of law placed upon them to produce identity papers. Yet, strangely enough, discourses of identity politics are complicit with a language that remains hostile to the foreigner.

---

53 J. Derrida, 'The Principle of Hospitality', *The Paper Machine*, trans. R. Bowlby (Stanford, CA: Stanford University Press, 2005), p. 67.

54 Caputo, *Deconstruction in an Nutshell*, p. 110.

Such discourse effectively closes the disjointure that provides the openness for justice to come, while at the same time inadequately distinguishes between or attends to specific connections that link the realms of politics, ethics and ontology. In positioning this book as working between a series of opposites that are indispensable for the articulation of the emancipatory promise – experience and knowledge, politics and philosophy, law and justice, self and other – I have aimed to open discourses of identity politics away from their propensity to become stuck within frames of self-reference. The consequences are gravely significant. The problems that have framed and troubled debates around identity for over three decades or more are not of an order that can be overcome. To invest identity politics with the task of overcoming essentialism, foundationalism and the gap between philosophy and politics, for instance, is to misunderstand the transformative potential that deconstruction brings to the chance for justice. The chance is always open to risk. It is not as if the emancipatory promise has a foreseeable destination. If it did, politics would be a matter of merely calculating the correct co-ordinates of a programme to set the promise on its course. If democracy is the current name used to guide the promise, it is precisely because the heritage of the concept contains within itself an openness and welcoming stance toward the Other that lends itself to the interminable task of responding to the promise. To send discourses of identity politics toward the stranger, then, is another way of reminding such discourses to maintain a space for the incalculable order of justice. This cannot be done by overcoming aporias (by definition an aporia is impassable and cannot be overcome), but by working between the impossibilities that structure the condition of possibility to *make* ethical decisions and render oneself open to the coming of something unheard of and new.

Bibliography

Agamben, G. *Homo Sacer: Sovereign Power and Bare Life*, trans. D. Heller Roazen (Stanford, CA: Stanford University Press, 1998).

Agamben, G. *State of Exception*, trans. K. Attell (Chicago, IL: University of Chicago Press, 2005).

Ahmad, A. 'Reconciling Derrida: "Spectres of Marx" and Deconstructive Politics', *New Left Review*, 208 (1994): 88–106.

Alcoff, L. 'Who's Afraid of Identity Politics?', in P. M. L. Moya and M. R. Hames-García (eds), *Reclaiming Identity Politics, Realist Theory and the Predicament of Postmodernism* (California: University of California Press, 2000), pp. 312–44.

Alcoff, L. *Visible Identities Race, Gender and The Self* (Oxford: Oxford University Press, 2006).

Alcoff, L. M., Hames-García, M. R., Mohanty, S. P. and Moya, P. M. L. (eds), *Identity Politics Reconsidered* (New York: Palgrave, 2006).

Altman, J. and Hinkson, M. *Coercive Reconciliation: Stabilise, Normalise, Exit Aboriginal Australia* (Melbourne: Arena Publications, 2007).

Arendt, H. *The Origins of Totalitarianism* (New York: Harcourt Brace Jovanovich, 1979).

Attwood, B. 'Comment on Hollinsworth', *Oceania*, 63, 2 (1992): 158–9.

Attwood, B. '"Learning About the Truth": The Stolen Generations Narrative', in B.Attwood and F. MacGowan (eds), *Telling Stories: Indigenous History and Memory in Australia and New Zealand* (Sydney: Allen and Unwin, 2001), pp. 183–212.

Attwood, B. 'Unsettling Pasts: Reconciliation and History in Settler Australia', *Postcolonial Studies*, 8, 3 (2005): 243–59.

Attwood, B. and Markus, A. *The 1967 Referendum: Race, Power and the Australian Constitution* (Canberra: Aboriginal Studies Press, 2007).

Badiou, A. 'Philosophy and the "Death of Communism"', trans. O. Feltham and J. Clemens, *Infinite Thought: Truth and the Return of Philosophy* (London and New York: Continuum, 2003).

Baker, K. M. and Reill, P. H. (eds) *What's Left of Enlightenment? A Postmodern Question* (Stanford, CA: Stanford University Press, 2001).

Banivanua-Mar, T. *Violence and Colonial Dialogue: The Australian-Pacific Indentured Labor Trade* (Honolulu: University of Hawaii Press, 2007).

Beckett, J. 'Comment on Hollinsworth', *Oceania,* 63, 2 (1992): 165–7.

Bennett, D. 'PC Panic, The Press and the Academy', *Meanjin: Cultural Difference and its Enemies*, 3 (Spring 1993): 435–46.

Bernauer, J. 'Foucault's Ecstatic Thinking', in J. Bernauer and D. Rasmussen (eds), *The Final Foucault* (Cambridge, MA and London: MIT Press, 1988), pp. 45–82.

Bernstein, R. 'Derrida: The Aporia of Forgiveness?', *Constellations*, 13, 3 (2006): 394–406.

Bird, C. (ed.) *The Stolen Generations: Their Stories* (Sydney: Random House, 1998).

Borradori, G. (ed.) *Philosophy in a Time of Terror: Dialogues with Jurgen Habermas and Jacques Derrida* (Chicago, IL: University of Chicago Press, 2003).

Bringing Them Home: Report of the National Inquiry into the Separation of Aboriginal and Torres Strait Islander Children from Their Families (Canberra: Commonwealth of Australia, 1997).

Briskman, L. *The Black Grapevine: Aboriginal Activism and the Stolen Generations* (Sydney: Federation Press, 2003).

Burnside, J. 'Stolen Generation: Time for Change', http://www.australiansall.com.au/stolen-generation-time-for-a-change/, accessed 11/10/2007.

Burnside, J. *Watching Brief: Reflections on Human Rights, Law and Justice* (Melbourne: Scribe, 2007).

Butler, J. *Gender Trouble: Feminism and the Subversion of Identity* (New York: Routledge, 1990).

Butler, J. *Bodies That Matter: On the Discursive Limits of Sex* (New York: Routledge, 1993).

Butler, J. 'Contingent Foundations: Feminism and the Question of "Postmodernism"', in L. Nicholson, S. Benhabib, J. Butler, D. Cornell and N. Fraser (eds), *Feminist Contentions: A Philosophical Exchange* (New York and London: Routledge, 1995), pp. 35–57.

Califia, P. *Sex Changes: The Politics of Transgenderism* (San Francisco, CA: Cleis Press, 2003) [1997].

Captuo, J. *Against Ethics: Contributions to a Poetics of Obligations with Constant Reference to Deconstruction* (Indianapolis: Indiana University Press, 1993).

Caputo, J. *Deconstruction in a Nutshell: A Conversation with Jacques Derrida* (New York: Fordham University Press, 1997).

Cornell, D. *The Philosophy of the Limit* (New York and London: Routledge, 1992).

Council for Aboriginal Reconciliation, *Australian Declaration Towards Reconciliation*, 2000. http://www.austlii.edu.au/au/other/IndigLRes/car/2000/12/pg3.htm.

Cowlishaw, G. 'Introduction: Representing Racial Issues', *Oceania*, 63, 3 (1993): 183–94.

Cunneen, C. and Grix, J. *The Limitations of Litigation in Stolen Generations Cases* (Canberra: Australian Institute of Aboriginal and Torres Strait Islander Studies, 2004).

de Man, P. 'Semiology and Rhetoric', in *Allegories of Reading: Figural Language in Rousseau, Nietzsche, Rilke, and Proust* (New Haven, CT: Yale University Press, 1979).

Denton, A. *Enough Rope*, ABC, 30/10/2006. Transcript available from http://www.abc.net.au/tv/enoughrope/transcripts/s1776670.htm.

Derrida, J. *Of Grammatology*, trans. G. Spivak (Baltimore and London: Johns Hopkins University Press, 1974).

Derrida, J. 'Cogito and the History of Madness', trans. A. Bass, in *Writing and Difference* (Chicago, IL: University of Chicago Press, 1978), pp. 31–63.

Derrida, J. 'Violence and Metaphysics: An Essay on the Thought of Emmanuel Levinas', trans. A. Bass, in *Writing and Difference* (Chicago, IL: University of Chicago Press, 1978), pp. 79–153 [1964].

Derrida, J. 'The Principle of Reason: The University in the Eyes of its Pupils', trans. C. Porter and E. P. Morris, *Diacritics*, 13, 3 (1983): 3–20.

Derrida, J. 'Afterword: Toward an Ethic of Discussion', *Limited Inc.*, ed. G. Graff (Evanston, IL: Northwestern University Press, 1988), pp. 111–60.

Derrida, J. 'At This Very Moment in This Work Here I am', trans. R. Berezdivin, in R. Bernasconi and S. Critchley (eds), *Re-Reading Levinas* (Bloomington and Indianapolis: Indiana University Press, 1991), pp. 11–48 [Fr. 1980].

Derrida, J. 'Force of Law: "The Mystical Foundation of Authority"', trans M. Quaintance, in D. Cornell, M. Rosenfeld and D.G. Carlson (eds), *Deconstruction and the Possibility of Justice* (New York and London: Routledge, 1992), pp. 3–67.

Derrida, J. 'Of an Apocalyptic Tone Recently Adopted in Philosophy', trans. P. Fenves, in P. Fenves, *Raising the Tone of Philosophy: Late Essays by Immanuel Kant, Transformative Critique by Jacques Derrida* (Baltimore, PA: Johns Hopkins University Press, 1993). pp. 117–71.

Derrida, J. *Specters of Marx: The State of the Debt, the Work of Mourning, and the New International*, trans. P. Kamuf (New York and London: Routledge, 1994).

Derrida, J. *Politics of Friendship*, trans. G. Collins (London, Verso, 1997).

Derrida, J. *On Cosmopolitanism and Forgiveness* (New York: Routledge, 2001).

Derrida, J. 'Autoimmunity: Real and Symbolic Suicide', in *Philosophy in a Time of Terror*, ed. G. Borradori (Chicago, IL: University of Chicago Press, 2003), pp. 85–136.

Derrida, J. *Rogues: Two Essays on Reason* (Stanford, CA: Stanford University Press, 2005).

Derrida, J. *The Paper Machine*, trans R. Bowlby (Stanford, CA: Stanford University Press, 2005).

Derrida, J. and Dufourmantelle, A. *Of Hospitality: Anne Dufourmantelle invites Jacques Derrida to Respond*, trans R. Bowlby (Stanford, CA: Stanford University Press, 2000).

Derrida, J. and McDonald, C. 'Choreographies', trans. C. McDonald, in *The Ear of the Other: Otobiography, Transference, Translation*, ed. C. McDonald (Lincoln and London: University of Nebraska Press, 1985), pp. 163–85 [1982].

Derrida, J. and Sprinker, M. 'Politics and Friendship: An Interview with Jacques Derrida', trans. Robert Harvey, in E. Ann Kaplan and Michael Sprinker (eds), *The Althusserian Legacy* (London and New York: Verso, 1993), pp. 182–231.

Downs. L. 'If Woman is Just an Empty Category, Then Why Am I Afraid to Walk Alone at Night? Identity Politics Meets the Postmodern Subject', *Comparative Study of Society and History*, 35 (Apr. 1993): 414–37.

Eagleton, T. 'Marxism Without Marxism', *Radical Philosophy*, 73 (1995): 35–7.

Eagleton, T. 'A Future for Socialism?', *Arena Journal*, 16, 1 (2000): 5–12.

Elder, C. *Being Australian: Narratives of National Identity* (Sydney: Allen and Unwin, 2007).

Fasuto-Sterling, A. 'The Five Sexes: Why Male and Female are not Enough', in S. la Font (ed.), *Constructing Sexualities: Readings in Sexuality, Gender and Culture* (Upper Saddle River, NJ: Prentice Hall, 2003), pp. 166–71.

Feldstein, R. *Political Correctness: A Response from the Cultural Left* (Minneapolis and London: University of Minnesota Press, 1997).

Flynn, B. 'Derrida and Foucault: Madness and Writing', in H. Silverman (ed.), *Continental Philosophy II: Derrida and Deconstruction* (New York and London: Routledge, 1989), pp. 201–18.

Foley, G. 'The Australian Labor Party and the *Native Title Act*', in Aileen Moreton Robinson (ed.), *Sovereign Subjects: Indigenous Sovereignty Matters* (Crows Nest: Allen & Unwin, 2007), pp. 118–39

Foucault, M. *Madness and Civilisation: A History of Insanity in the Age of Reason*, trans. R. Howard (London: Routledge, 1967) [Fr. 1961].

Foucault, M. *The Archaeology of Knowledge*, trans. A. M. Sheridan Smith (London and New York: Tavistock, 1972) [Fr 1969].

Foucault, M. 'What is an Author?', trans. D. F. Bouchard and S. Simon, in *Language, Counter Memory and Practice: Selected Essays and Interviews by Michel Foucault*, ed. D. F. Bouchard (New York: Cornell University Press, 1977), pp. 113–38 [Fr. 1969].

Foucault, M. 'The Order of Discourse', trans. I. McLeod, in Robert Young (ed.), *Untying the Text: A Post-Structuralist Reader* (Boston: Routledge and Kegan Paul, 1981), pp. 51–77 [Fr.1970].

Foucault, M. *The History of Sexuality: An Introduction*, trans. R. Hurley (Harmondsworth: Penguin, 1978) [Fr. 1976].

Foucault, M. 'Nietzsche, Genealogy, History', trans. D. F. Bouchard and S. Somin, in *The Foucault Reader*, ed., P. Rabinow (Harmondsworth: Penguin, 1984), pp. 76–100 [Fr. 1971].

Foucault, M. 'On the Genealogy of Ethics: An Overview of Work in Progress', trans. C. Porter, in *The Foucault Reader*, ed. P. Rabinow (Harmondsworth: Penguin, 1984), pp. 340–72.

Foucault, M. 'What is Enlightenment?', trans. C. Porter, in *The Foucault Reader*, ed P. Rabinow (Harmondsworth: Penguin, 1984), pp. 32–50.

Foucault, M. *The Use of Pleasure: Volume 2: The History of Sexuality*, trans. R. Hurley (New York: Vintage Books, 1985) [Fr. 1984].

Foucault, M. *The Care of the Self: Volume 3: The History of Sexuality*, trans R. Hurley (Harmondsworth: Penguin, 1986).

Foucault, M. 'Politics and the Study of Discourse', trans. C. Gordon, in G. Burchell, C. Gordon and P. Miller (eds), *The Foucault Effect: Studies in Governmentality* (Chicago, IL: University of Chicago Press, 1991), pp. 53–72 [Fr. 1972].

Foucault, M. and Deleuze, G. 'Intellectuals and Power: A Conversation between M. Foucault and G. Deleuze', trans. D. F. Bouchard and S. Simon, in *Language, Counter Memory, Practice*, ed. D. F. Bouchard (New York: Cornell University Press, 1977), pp. 205–17.

Frow J. 'What Was Postmodernism?' (Sydney: Local Consumption Occasional Paper, no. 11, 1991).

Frow, J. 'A Politics of Stolen Time', *Meanjin*, 57, 2 (1998): 351–67.

Fuss, D. *Essentially Speaking: Feminism, Nature and Difference* (New York and London: Routledge, 1989).

Gasché, R. *The Tain of the Mirror: Derrida and the Philosophy of Reflection* (Cambridge, MA: Harvard University Press, 1988).

Gay, P. *The Party of Humanity: Studies in the French Enlightenment* (London: Weidenfeld and Nicolson, 1964).

Gelder, K. and Jacobs, J. M. *Uncanny Australia: Sacredness and Identity in a Postcolonial Nation* (Melbourne: Melbourne University Press, 1998.

Gooder, H. and Jacobs, J. M. 'Belonging and non-Belonging: the Apology in a Reconciling Nation', in A. Blunt and C. McEwan (eds), *Postcolonial Geographies* (New York: Continuum, 2002), pp. 200–13.

Habermas, J. 'Modernity – An Incomplete Project', trans. S. Benhabib, in H. Foster (ed.), *Postmodern Culture* (London and Sydney: Pluto Press, 1983), pp. 3–15.

Haebich, A. *Broken Circles: Fragmenting Indigenous Families 1800-2000* (Fremantle: Arts Press, 2001).

Halperin, D. *Saint Foucault: Towards a Gay Hagiography* (Oxford: Oxford University Press, 1996).

Halwani, R. 'Prolegomena to Any Future Metaphysics of Sexual Identity: Recasting the Essentialism and Social Constructionism Debate', in L. M. Alcoff, M. R. Hames-García, S. P. Mohanty and P. M. L. Moya (eds), *Identity Politics Reconsidered* (New York: Palgrave, 2006), pp. 209–27.

Haraway, D. 'A Cyborg Manifesto: Science, Technology and Socialist Feminism in the Late Twentieth Century', in E. Weed (ed.), *Coming to Terms: Feminism, Theory and Politics* (New York and London: Routledge, 1989), pp. 173–204.

Haraway, D. 'The Biopolitics of Postmodern Bodies: Constitutions of Self in Immune System Discourse', in *Simians, Cyborgs and Women: The Reinvention of Nature* (London: Free Association Books, 1991), pp. 203–30.

Harding, S. (ed.) *The Feminist Standpoint Reader: Intellectual and Political Controversies* (New York and London: Routledge, 2004).

Harding, S. 'Transformation vs. Resistance Identity Projects: Epistemological Resources for Social Justice Movements', in L. M. Alcoff, M. R. Hames-García, S. P. Mohanty and P. M. L. Moya (eds), *Identity Politics Reconsidered* (New York: Palgrave, 2006), pp. 246–63.

Hokari, M. 'Globalising Aboriginal Reconciliation: Indigenous Australians and Asian (Japanese) Migrants', *Cultural Studies Review*, 9 (2003): 84–101.

Hollinsworth, D. 'Coagulating Categories: A Reply to Responses', *Oceania*, 63, 2 (1992): 168–71.

Hollinsworth, D. 'Discourses on Aboriginality and the Politics of Identity in Australia', *Oceania*, 63, 2 (1992): 137–55.

Hunt, E. K. *History of Economic Thought: A Critical Perspective* (California: Wadsworth Publishing Company, 1979).

Jay, M. *Songs of Experience: Modern American and European Variations on a Universal Theme* (University of California Press, 2005).

Kamuf, P. 'Replacing Feminist Criticism', in E. F. Keller and M. Hirsch (eds), *Conflicts in Feminism* (New York: Routledge, 1990), pp. 105–11 [1981].

Kamuf, P. *The Division of Literature or The University in Deconstruction* (Chicago and London: University of Chicago Press, 1997).

Kamuf, P. 'Experience', *English Studies in Canada*, Dec. (2004): 3-4, Academic Research Library, pp. 24–9.

Kamuf, P. *Book of Addresses* (Stanford, CA: Stanford University Press, 2005).

Kant, I. 'An Answer to the Question: What is Enlightenment?', trans. H. B. Nisbet, in *Kant's Political Writings*, ed. H. Reiss (Cambridge: Cambridge University Press, 1970), pp. 54–60.

Kant, I. 'On a Newly Arisen Superior Tone in Philosophy', trans. P. Fenves, *Raising the Tone of Philosophy: Late Essays by Immanuel Kant, Transformative Critique by Jacques Derrida* (Baltimore and London: Johns Hopkins University Press, 1993), pp. 51–81.

Kessler, S. 'The Medical Construction of Gender: Case Management of Intersexed Infants', *Signs: Journal of Women in Culture and Society*, 16, 1 (1990): 3–26.

Kessler, S. and McKenna, W. 'Who put the "Trans" in Transgender? Gender Theory and Everyday Life', in S. la Font (ed.), *Constructing Sexualities: Readings in Sexuality, Gender and Culture* (Upper Saddle River, NJ: Prentice Hall, 2003), pp. 223–6.

Kordvani, A. 'Hospitality, Politics of Mobility, and Movement of Service Suppliers under the GATS', *Melbourne Journal of International Law*, 7 (2006): 74–103.

La Capra, 'Experience and Identity', in L. M. Alcoff, M. R. Hames-García, S. P. Mohanty and P. M. L. Moya (eds), *Identity Politics Reconsidered* (New York: Palgrave, 2006), pp. 228–45.

Laclau, E. 'The Time is out of Joint', *Diacritics*, 25, 2 (1995): 86–96.

Laclau, E. and Mouffe, C. *Hegemony and Socialist Strategy: Towards a Radical Democratic Politics*, trans. W. Moore and P. Cammack (London, Verso, 1985).

Lake, M and Reynolds, H. *Drawing the Global Colour Line: White Men's Countries and the Question of Racial Equality* (Melbourne: Melbourne University Press, 2008), pp. 137–65

Langton, M. '*Well, I heard it on the radio and I saw it on the television: An essay for the Australian Film Commission on the politics and aesthetics of filmmaking by and about Aboriginal people and things*' (Woolloomooloo: Australian Film Commission, 1993): 23–43.

Lattas, A. 'Wiping the Blood off Aboriginality: The Politics of Aboriginal Embodiment in Contemporary Intellectual Debate', *Oceania*, 63, 2 (1992): 160–64.

Lattas, A. 'Essentialism, Memory and Resistance: Aboriginality and the Politics of Authenticity', *Oceania*, 63, 3 (1993): 240–67.

Laurie, V. 'Blacks Question "Aboriginal" Writer', *The Weekend Australian*, 20–21 July (1996): 1, 12.

Laurie, V. 'Identity Crisis', *Australian Magazine* in *The Weekend Australian*, 20–21 July (1996): 28–32.

Lehman, G. 'Authentic and Essential: A Review of Anita M Heiss' Dhuuluu-Yala (To Talk Straight): Publishing Indigenous Literature', *Australian Humanities Review*, 33, (2004), accessed 28 December 2006, http://www.lib.latrobe.edu.au/AHR/archive?Issue-August-2004/lehman.html.

Levinas, E. *Totality and Infinity*, trans. A. Lingis (Pittsburgh, PA: Duequesne University Press, 1969).

Levinas, E. 'Dialogue with Emmanuel Levinas', in R. Cohen (ed.), *Face to Face with Levinas* (New York: State University of New York Press, 1986).

Levinas, E. 'At This Very Moment in This Work Here I am', trans. R. Berezdivin, in R. Bernasconi and S. Critchley (eds), *Re-Reading Levinas* (Bloomington and Indianapolis: Indiana University Press, 1991), pp. 11–48 [Fr. 1980].

'Library offers, imam, gypsy, gay person for "loan"', 17 August 2005, accessed 13 October 2006 http://www.abc.net.au/news/newsitems/200508/s1439257.htm.

Lucy, N. *Debating Derrida* (Carlton: Melbourne University Press, 1995).

Lyotard, J.-F. *The Postmodern Condition: A Report on Knowledge*, trans. G. Bennington and B. Masumi (Minneapolis: University of Minnesota Press, 1984).

McHoul, A. and Grace, W. *A Foucault Primer: Discourse, Power and the Subject* (Carlton: Melbourne University Press, 1993).

Manne, R. *In Denial: The Stolen Generations and the Right* (Melbourne: Black Inc., 2001).

Manne, R. 'The Road to Tampa', in L. Jayasuriya, D. Walker and J. Gothard (eds), *Legacies of White Australia* (Perth: University of Western Australia Press, 2003), pp. 163–94.

Manne, R. with Corlett, D. *Sending Them Home: Refugees and the New Politics of Indifference*, Quarterly Essay 13 (Melbourne: Black Inc., 2004).

Markus, A. 'Of Continuities and Discontinuities: Reflections on a Century of Australian Immigration Control', in L. Jayasuriya, D. Walker and J. Gothard (eds), *Legacies of White Australia* (Perth: University of Western Australia Press, 2003), pp. 175–89.

Marr, D. 'Escape from Life in Limbo', *Sydney Morning Herald*, 27 October 2007. http://www.smh.com.au/news/national/escape-from-a-life-in-limbo/2007/10/26/1192941339538.html.

Marx, K. 'Theses on Feuerbach', trans. G. Benton in *Early Writings: Marx* (Harmondsworth: Penguin, 1974), pp. 421–3. Thesis XI appears on p. 423 [G. 1845].

Marx, K. 'The Eighteenth Brumaire of Louis Bonaparte', in *The Marx–Engels Reader* ed. R. C. Tucker (New York: W. W. Norton, 1972), pp. 436–525 [G. 1852].

Marx, K. and Engels, F. 'The German Ideology', trans. C. Dutt, W. Lough, C. P. Magill, in *Collected Works, Vol. 5: Marx and Engels: 1845–1847* (London: Lawrence and Wishart, 1976), pp. 19–539 [G. 1845/1846].

Marx, K. and Engels, F. 'Manifesto of the Communist Party', in *The Marx–Engels Reader*, ed. R. C. Tucker (New York: W. W. Norton, 1972), pp. 331–62 [G. 1848].

Mickler, S. *The Myth of Privilege: Aboriginal Status, Media Visions, Public Ideas* (Fremantle: Fremantle Arts Press, 1998).

Morton, J. 'Race, Reciprocity, Reconciliation: Stolen Children and the Elementary Structures of Justice in Australia', unpublished manuscript.

Naas, M. '"One Nation … Indivisible": Jacques Derrida on the Autoimmunity of Democracy and Sovereignty of God', *Research in Phenomenology*, 36 (2006): 15–44.

Nelson, B. 'Text of Brendan Nelson's "sorry" response', *The Age*, 13 February 2008, http://www.theage.com.au/news/national/bfull-textb-brendan-nelsons-speech/20 08/02/13/1202760363287.html.

Nicholson, L. S., Benhabib, S., Butler, J., Cornell, D. and Fraser, N. (eds) *Feminist Contentions: A Philosophical Exchange* (New York and London: Routledge, 1995).

Nicolacopoulos, T. and Vassilacopoulos, G. 'On the Other side of Xenophobia: Philoxenia as the Ground of Refugee Rights', *Australian Journal of Human Rights*, 17 (2004), http://www.austlii.edu.au/au/journals/AJHR/2004/17.html

Norris, C. *The Truth About Postmodernism* (Oxford and Massachusetts: Blackwell, 1993).

Nyoongah, M. 'Self-determining Our Aboriginality: A Response to "Discourses on Aboriginality and the Politics of Identity in Urban Australia"', *Oceania*, 63, 2 (1992): 156–7.

Patton, P. 'Mabo and Australian Society: Towards a Postmodern Republic', *The Australian Journal of Anthropology*, 6, 12 (Aug. 1995): 83–94.

Peperzak, A. *To the Other: An Introduction to the Philosophy of Emmanuel Levinas* (Indiana: Purdue University Press, 1993).

Reynolds, H. *Aboriginal Sovereignty: Reflections on Race, State and Nation* (Sydney: Allen and Unwin, 1996).

Reynolds, H. *Why Weren't We Told?: A Personal Search for the Truth About our History* (Melbourne: Viking, 1999).

Reynolds, H. *The Other Side of the Frontier: Aboriginal Resistance to the European Invasion of Australia* (Sydney: University of New South Wales Press, 2007) [1981].

Rudd, K. 'Apology to Australia's Indigenous People', House of Representatives, Parliament House, Canberra, 13 February 2008 http://www.pm.gov.au/media/ Speech/2008/speech_0073.cfm

Schapp, A. 'The Proto-politics of Reconciliation: Lefort and the Aporia of Forgiveness in Arendt and Derrida', *Australian Journal of Political Science*, 41 (Dec. 2006): 615–30.

Scott, J. 'Experience', in J. Butler and J. Scott (eds), *Feminists Theorize The Political* (New York: Routledge, 1992), pp. 22–40.

Soper, K. 'The Limits of Hauntology', *Radical Philosophy*, 75 (1996): 26–31.

Spivak, G. 'Subaltern Studies: Deconstructing Historiography', *Other Worlds: Essays in Cultural Politics* (New York and London: Routledge, 1987), pp. 197–221.

Spivak, G. 'Can the Subaltern Speak?', in G. Nelson and L. Grossberg (eds), *Marxism and the Interpretation of Culture* (London: Macmillan, 1988), pp. 271–373.

Spivak, G. 'More on Power/Knowledge', in *Outside in the Teaching Machine* (New York and London: Routledge, 1993), pp. 25–51.

Spivak, G. and Rooney, E. 'In a Word: *Interview*', in G. Spivak, *Outside in the Teaching Machine* (New York and London: Routledge, 1993), pp. 1–23.

Sprinker, M (ed.) *Ghostly Demarcations: A Symposium on Jacques Derrida's 'Specters of Marx'* (London and New York: Verso, 1999).

Stanner, W. E. H. *The 1968 Boyer Lectures: After the Dreaming* (Sydney: The Australian Broadcasting Commission, 1969).

Terry, 'Theorizing Deviant Historiography', *differences*, 3, 2 (1991): 55–74.

Toews, J. 'Intellectual History after the Linguistic Turn: The Autonomy of Meaning and the Irreducibility of Experience', *American Historical Review*, 92 (1987): 879–907.

UNHCR. 'Global Trends 2006: Refugees, Asylum Seekers, Returnees, Internally Displaced and Stateless Persons', Division of Operational Services, July 2007. http://www.unhcr.org/statistics/STATISTICS/4676a71d4.pdf.

Walby, S. 'Complexity Theory, Systems Theory and Multiple Intersecting Social Inequalities', *Philosophy of the Social Sciences*, 37, 4 (2007): 449–70.

Wilchins, R. 'A Certain Kind of Freedom: Power and the Truth of Bodies – Four Essays on Gender', in J. Nestle, C. Howell and R. Wilchins (eds), *GENDERqUEER: Voices from Beyond the Sexual Binary* (Los Angeles and New York: Alyson Books, 2002), pp. 23–63.

Wilkerson, W. 'Is There Something You Need to Tell Me? Coming Out and the Ambiguity of Experience', in P. M. L. Moya and M. R. Hames-García (eds), *Reclaiming Identity Politics, Realist Theory and the Predicament of Postmodernism* (California: University of California Press, 2000), pp. 251–78.

Williams, J. (ed.) *PC Wars: Politics and Theory in the Academy* (New York: Routledge, 1995).

Young, I. M. *Inclusion and Democracy* (Oxford: Oxford University Press, 2002).

Zammito, J. 'Reading Experience: The Debate in Intellectual History among Scott, Toews and La Capra', in P. M. L. Moya and M. R. Hames-García (eds), *Reclaiming Identity Politics, Realist Theory and the Predicament of Postmodernism* (California: University of California Press, 2000), pp. 279–311.

Index